The Kindness of Children

VIVIAN GUSSIN PALEY

The Kindness of Children

HARVARD UNIVERSITY PRESS

Cambridge, Massachusetts and London, England

Third printing, 1999

Library of Congress Cataloging-in-Publication Data

Paley, Vivian Gussin, 1929–
The kindness of children / Vivian Gussin Paley.
    p.   cm.
ISBN 0-674-50358-9 (alk. paper)
1. Kindness.   2. Storytelling—Psychological aspects.
3. Interpersonal relations in children.   4. Interpersonal
communication in children.   5. Paley, Vivian Gussin, 1929–
I. Title.
BJ1533.K5P34   1999
305.234—dc21   98-37322

Designed by Gwen Nefsky Frankfeldt

To my mother, Yetta Meisel Gussin

The moral universe rests upon
the breath of schoolchildren

RABBI YEHUDA NISIAH
CIRCA 250 C.E.

Time and place have lost their markers for me. The first Monday in September is supposed to end the summer and I should be in school preparing for a new group of children. But that was in another life when my name seemed permanently affixed to a kindergarten door. The days still begin with the expectation that something significant will happen, but there is no pattern I recognize and the pages of my notebook fill more slowly.

This morning, for example, my dog and I suddenly take cover behind a patch of tall dune grass while a great blue heron performs its dainty rituals in the pink-tinted dawn. When Cass sees the heron dancing at the shoreline, a ridge of fur mobilizes down his back and he refuses to move forward. So here we sit while I count the heron's steps: two up, two back, wing flutter, wing flutter, and repeat.

Perhaps it is the emptiness of the beach that heightens the heron's ghostly effect. Most of the houses are shuttered, their owners returned to Milwaukee, Rockford, Chicago, and St. Louis. I have come to this densely wooded peninsula to learn to write of something other than the children in my classes, but the transition is not smooth.

The stately heron possessively scans each approaching wave and I think of Harry coveting the blocks, Harry screaming his bad talk, fighting over every inch of territory. Grabbing and pushing, hot tears steaming up his glasses and matting down a shock of red hair, his epithets left me shaking. "Leave this be, you fucking idiots! Can't you see I need to do this by my *own*self?"

Yet later—how can one explain this?—he would draw pictures of animals running free and there were no storm clouds in his stories. "The sun is shining," he dictated to me one day. "The sun is shining. The puppies are playing and the sun is shining."

As if entering Harry's idyllic scene, the heron undulates its graceful neck toward the first rays of sunlight, looking like something Harry might have crayoned, an uninterrupted line of life and motion. How contented Harry would be on this beach, his castles impervious to the whims of others. The tides would come and go, but if there were time to complete his work by his "own-self," perhaps that would have been enough.

The unfinished business of the classroom pursues me. I long to describe the bark of the red pine and the pale yellow mushrooms dotting the forest floor but classroom scenes intrude. I want to celebrate the fiery ball about to burst through the horizon and instead see the anguish in Harry's face and feel it in mine. The jailed and the jailor.

The heron is completely still now, one leg suspended in midair. Then, spreading a huge expanse of wing, it skims over the rolling foam, dipping its head to capture the fish of its choice. As deftly as Harry would seize the perfect block.

In a swift grey blur, the heron swoops upwards until it is beyond the tallest pine at the top of the dunes. Fingers of scarlet and orange cross its path like a divine hand carrying it aloft. Harry's crayon would be off the paper at this point and I can hear my automatic warning, "Please don't mark up the table, Harry!"

In October, I travel to London to address a group of schoolteachers. They might be interested in Harry and the heron but I've lost the urgency of the connections I made that day on the beach. I seem unable to grasp life's deeper meaning in the behaviors of herons or mushrooms. Only a classroom of children can organize my experiences into a story. Like a child, without a story I cannot explain myself.

On the morning of my talk, I visit a nearby nursery school attended by children of many backgrounds, but on this day another sort of child has come. Every Friday a small group arrives from a school for severely disabled children. None is able to walk or even sit unaided. They are pushed in wheelchairs or carried by teachers.

These four- and five-year-olds have come to be with ordinary children. Just to be with them, no miracles expected. A boy named Teddy sits strapped into a wheelchair, his head protected by a thickly padded helmet. This is the second time he has come to Miss Eliot's classroom and apparently he remembers that after the storybook is read the children are allowed to play.

Teddy stares ahead as if he cannot see. However, the moment the book is closed he turns to the young woman beside him, his head bobbing dangerously. He wants to say something, but it will not be easy. The effort begins in his torso, wrenches through twitching shoulders and flinging arms until at last a single word emerges. "Car?" he asks.

His teacher smiles at him and leaves the room, returning soon pulling a small red car into which Teddy is strapped and cushioned. A complex arrangement of pulleys enables him to inch along by himself and he pedals to a group of children playing store among a collection of wooden crates and empty food containers. Once again, Teddy contorts his small frame in order to speak. "Crispies," he whispers, extending a hand as if it contains money.

The Indian child at the toy cash register waits patiently for Teddy's request, watching him closely the entire time. How easily the children do this; even the most impulsive child is not uncomfortable with awkward mannerisms in others. Children are deeply curious about odd behaviors and seldom offended or worried by them. What a remarkable gift to bestow upon another person, it occurs to me, and so difficult for adults to accomplish.

The boy pretends to take money from Teddy and, in exchange, gives him two little cereal boxes, saying, in a clipped accent, "Here you go, sir. Two for the price of one!" It is a simple transaction, such as might be seen any place where children play, but the joy it brings to Teddy's face fills my eyes with tears. What could I ever do to cause him to gaze at me that way?

The sudden conviction that I am witnessing a sacred

ritual is unnerving. I want to remain inside this scene, watching Teddy's face, but I am summoned into the teacher's lounge for tea and conversation. By the time I return, Teddy is back in his wheelchair, passive and withdrawn. However, he will be allowed to stay for one more activity, something he has not seen before, and the events of the morning will take on new layers of significance for him—and for me.

Several children have dictated stories to Miss Eliot, which they are about to dramatize with classmates. In the first, two sisters find a bunny and take it home, a basic doll-corner plot, but Teddy is startled. His eyes open wide and his body begins to tremble. Pleading wordlessly, he reaches a quivering arm toward his teacher.

Edmond approaches them. His story is next. "Your little boy needs his car," he says. "He wants to be in my story." Edmond's story is about a baby bear, a crocodile, and a puppy frightened by a monster. "Your little boy could be the puppy."

The teacher is kind but also tired. "I'm sorry, it's too late," she tells him. "The van is packed for us to leave."

Teddy retreats into his cushions but by now others are crowded around. "He can't do this without his car, you know," they urge. "He wants to move by himself. We could bring him the car."

A look of astonishment spreads over Teddy's face. Can a boy in a padded helmet really have friends like these who need him in their stories and in their play? Lisa, a Chinese girl, takes Teddy's hand. "Pretend you're the puppy and you didn't learn to walk yet."

Teddy's teacher pushes his wheelchair onto the rug and the children surround him as the story is acted out. I cannot see his face but his muted cry follows the monster's growl.

After the van leaves, I sit at a lunch table with Edmond and four classmates. They glance my way shyly, waiting for me to speak. "In my kindergarten," I begin, "we also act out each other's stories, just as you do."

"With bad guys and monsters?" asks the boy from India.

"The boys like bad guys and monsters," I reply. "Hardly ever the girls."

"That's the same as us!" Edmond shouts. "What else do the boys do?"

"I'll tell you about one boy. His name is Harry and he always wants to build alone in the blocks." How odd for me to speak here of Harry, yet I really do wonder how these children feel about him. "He becomes upset and even fights if anyone tries to help him."

"That's like Rudy," a girl tells me, pointing to a blond boy at the next table. "Our teacher says Rudy needs his space. Because he has special ideas that's private to himself."

"And he cries and squeezes us," Edmond adds. "Miss Eliot says let him have the blocks for a while after lunch and don't bother him. That will make him happy."

I watch Miss Eliot leaning over Rudy, explaining something in low tones. How does she know he needs his space, as does the heron, if he is to capture the prize and fly above the trees? Furthermore, why is she so certain, when others are not, that the children will want Rudy to soar heavenward every day after lunch? It must have not surprised her at all when the children begged Teddy's teacher to let them retrieve the little red car so he could move by himself.

Walking to my hotel, a curious notion enters my mind. When God promises Abraham not to destroy the wicked cities of Sodom and Gomorrah if even ten righteous people can be found, how differently the biblical tale might have ended had Abraham searched in Miss Eliot's classroom.

Teddy hovers over me, out of reach. When I had my own classroom, the children and I kept track of the ongoing narrative as though we were characters in a novel, repeating each other's words, expanding the plot. Sometimes an event bound us together in such harmony that for a while we seemed to step to a single rhythm. We made rituals of these experiences hoping to recapture the original feelings, building our classroom culture layer upon layer.

Now the Teddy incident resounds in the same way, but there is no context in which to place the melody. However, two weeks later, in a California fourth-grade classroom, Teddy enters the conversation. I have been demonstrating the same kind of storytelling and acting he watched so intently in a London nursery school, and it seems natural to speak of Teddy into whom the stories breathed life itself.

From the moment I begin to describe him, a silence descends. The children's faces reflect Teddy's every joy and sorrow. Manuel asks, "Did they bring Teddy his car?" I shake my head. "No, they didn't. It was time to leave." The children's disappointment is visible; the effect of the story I have just told goes far beyond my expectations.

"I knew they wouldn't," Lucy says. "But, anyway, can you tell that story again?" Her request surprises me; I feel a sense of intimacy with my audience as I repeat Teddy's story and try to recall my exact words. "Those are nice kids," someone says and Manuel whispers, "I love Teddy." Then, in a louder voice, "If I was in that school, I'd get Teddy his car, even before anyone could stop me."

"Me too," Luis says wistfully, but then he alters the course. "Sometimes people isn't that nice. They move away in the middle of what I try to tell them. Even I had a teacher to do this."

Marianne agrees quickly. "Yeah, people start doing something and they don't even care if I'm there. That makes me sad. And they think I'm lying, like when I say the ball didn't touch me and it really didn't 'cause I'd know if it did! They act like someone else is nicer than me, to believe them, not me."

Lucy is moved by Marianne's complaint. "*You* don't do that, Marianne!" she calls out. "Everyone remembers, huh?" She looks around the room. "When I came last year and didn't know English? She told me everything the teacher said, *everything*. And even when it was her turn to be leader with the jump rope she said, 'Let Lucy have a turn!'"

I cannot mask my excitement. "But this is what happened to my mother almost ninety years ago!" I exclaim. The opportunity to connect my mother to Lucy—and somehow to Teddy—gives me a light and airy feeling.

The children study my face, trying to imagine what I am about to reveal. "When my mother came from Russia she spoke no English. They put her in a first-grade room even though she was your age, but every day a fourth grader named Masha came to help her. She translated everything into Yiddish for my mother and then back into English. We're Jewish, you see, and Yiddish is the language my mother spoke."

"Did you know I come from Mexico?" Lucy asks. "So does lots of people here. But some people are Anglo like you and our teacher." Mrs. Phillips acknowledges the fact with a smile.

I sit down at an empty desk next to Lucy. "You're lucky," I say. "Now you speak English *and* Spanish. My mother also learned her new language. Masha came even when she didn't have to because she wanted my mother to speak English quickly and move to the fourth grade. This is a big favor to do for someone."

"Luis does favors too!" Carlos says, with a stammer. "If I don't have a partner he tells me okay. Some guys they never do this." He directs his gaze at a boy in the back who sticks out his tongue and crosses his eyes. Mrs. Phillips rises part way in her seat and casts a forbidding look.

Luis pays no attention to the drama going on behind

him. He has a question for me. "Why do you tell us that Teddy story? Are you a storyteller? You do that?"

"I don't call myself a storyteller, Luis. You're the first group I've told about Teddy. But he's been on my mind. Maybe I thought if you knew how much Teddy wanted to be in Edmond's story that would explain something about the storytelling and acting, especially the acting."

Luis is not satisfied. "Don't you tell mean stories, too? Because lots of times we're mean. I'm mean to my brothers and they're meaner to me."

"Sure, around here is mostly mean," Marianne nods. Why do she and Luis, who have just been complimented, feel they must set the record straight? "Like on the news," she continues, "or when we're bad and people get into trouble. But anyway, I like good stories better, like Teddy, and your mother." She turns to a black-haired girl. "Carmelita! Tell her about Jimmy, okay? About your knee?"

Everyone looks at a large boy in the back of the room while Carmelita stands uncertainly. "He's included," she confides and I can barely hear her. "That means he used to be in a special room but mostly now he's in our room, 'cept on Tuesday, I think."

Jimmy, in fact, has done his best *not* to be included

during my visit, humming to himself and getting up and down to look out of the window, where he stands now even as Carmelita talks about him. She raises her voice, making sure Jimmy can hear her. "See, one time he was running around yelling, he does that sometimes, and he pushed me down. My leg was bleeding, my knee was." Jimmy returns to his seat, watching Carmelita through heavily lidded eyes.

"So then Jimmy started really crying because I was hurt. And so he helped me get up and he took me to the teacher and he kept saying he was sorry and when it was lunch he gave me his Twinkie." Carmelita beams at Jimmy. "I'm telling about a good thing you did," she says quietly, but her hero does not respond.

I glance at the teacher, wondering if it is time to stop, but Luis is waving his hand and she calls on him. "Don't you know any bad stories?" he insists, and poor Harry pops into my mind, as though I must do penance for past deeds.

"There is a boy named Harry," I begin, "but maybe I'm the mean one here." Once again it seems odd to bring up these issues, Harry in the blocks and Rudy who is allowed his private time. However, it is the sort of thing I'd be doing in my own classroom or with older students who stopped by to visit.

Luis follows every detail. "How come Harry couldn't have private time?" He repeats "private time" as if he now has a name for something he may have imagined in a dream. "Because you're supposed to share, right?" Luis stands up and walks around, reminding me of my grandson who would pace the room when he began an important explanation.

"My uncle thinks a person needs to be alone sometimes," Luis says. "He tells my brothers, 'Let Luis do this by himself, you guys make him too sad.' He used to do that to our father, see, he made him too sad, and he's sorry, and now it's too late."

"Do you listen to your uncle, Luis?"

"Yeah, we're nicer when he's there." Luis returns to his seat and does not seem surprised to find Jimmy occupying half of it. The boys squeeze together for a moment, then Luis whispers to Jimmy who gets up and brings another chair, placing it next to Luis.

"What would your uncle do about Harry?" I ask, and Luis answers so promptly it is clear he and his uncle speak of such things. "He'd figure out if Harry is sad, you know, maybe his father is dead or he's in jail, something bad. Let him have a breather, that's what my uncle says. A breather. You know, let him be happy now, and then later he'll make you happy." Luis's words have great meaning for his classmates, most of whom know his uncle, a teacher in the school.

Thinking about Harry I feel guilty. "By the way, I forgot to tell you," I say to the class, "Harry did make us happy. He'd draw pictures of animals running so fast they seemed to fly and he told stories like this one: 'The sun is shining, the sun is shining, the puppies are playing and the sun is shining.'"

Jimmy is at my side, tugging my sleeve. "Is that the little kid the one that fights said that?" I nod and he careens toward his seat, bumping into two chairs as he goes. I stare after him, startled by the gift he has given me, the gift of listening to my story and responding to it. I must return the favor.

"Jimmy, wait!" I blurt out. "Wait! One more thing about Harry. You'll want to hear this." Jimmy reverses himself in midstride, his arms swinging loosely at his side.

I speak rapidly, wanting to secure his attention, but it is not necessary. He wants to hear more about Harry. "One day, as usual, I was furious with him. He'd been racing down the hall, way ahead of the class, and I was yelling at him to come back, even though I'd promised myself never to do that anymore. Suddenly he stops in front of a boy sitting on a bench near a second-grade classroom. It is Martin, someone Harry fights with all the time, on the playground, even passing in the hall. One insult leads to another and they're pounding on each other."

Jimmy stands before me, stock-still, concentrating on my story. "Harry asked Martin why he was sitting there but Martin wouldn't answer. He kept his head down. Maybe he was crying, I don't know."

"That kid was punished," Luis says and several children nod knowingly. Jimmy seems alarmed; I wonder if I have chosen the wrong story but it is too late to stop.

"Yes, I'm sure he was, but I thought Harry might punch him for not answering so I grabbed his hand and walked back to the room, criticizing him all the time. Harry waited for me to finish, then he said, 'Why is Martin on that bench?' I told him that Martin must have done something to make his teacher really angry. Harry snapped his head up at me, his eyes huge and frightened. 'So he has to sit alone in the hall? You *do* that?'"

The children wait for my answer. This rather ordinary story has gripped them more than I expected. It was Jimmy I had in mind when I began but the others are equally absorbed. "'No, *I* don't do that,' I told him, 'but a few teachers might, not too many.'" Jimmy relaxes; the "not too many" reassures him.

"Let me tell you, Harry was grim," I continue. "For a while he just stuck to my side. Then he did something remarkable. He ran to the snack table, snatched up *his* share, two oatmeal raisin cookies—his favorites, by the way—and was down the hall before I could say 'Don't run!' A few minutes later he was back, without the cookies, laughing and punching the air. 'Hey, guess what Martin said?' Harry shouted. '"Hey, man!" That's what he said, and he was laughing like anything. "Hey, man!" That's what he told me!'"

All the while I've been telling the story, Jimmy has been moving toward me until he is close enough to touch. "Do you like Harry now?" he asks me. I hold out my hand and Jimmy takes it. "I do, Jimmy. I like Harry a lot."

I bring such stories as these to my mother, who still remembers the things I told her when I was in first grade. She is ninety-seven and lives alone now in a residential hotel for older people, seldom leaving her studio apartment except to go downstairs for meals.

"It's no use my going out, even to shul," she tells me.

"I can barely hear or see the rabbi. It's all a blur. Even the dining room is a problem. The echoes are like thunder and my hearing aids make it worse." When my husband and I urge her to move in with us, she is surprised. "Why? I like it here, by myself. There is time to think."

A prayer book and Torah are open on the table in front of her. She insists she is not a religious person, but every day she reads fragments of the familiar texts, a word or two at a time, using a strong magnifying lens. Sometimes she'll ask me to copy a quotation into large print so she can refer to it more easily. "Here, Vivian, at the top. Do you have time to do this? It's from Micah."

She knows the words of the ancient prophet by heart and it gives her pleasure to see them boldly highlighted: "It has been told thee what is good and what the Lord doth require of thee," she recites. "Only to do justly, and to love mercy, and to walk humbly with thy God." My mother finds the place on the page, using her lens. "Start with the first line, 'It has been told thee, O Man.'"

"IT HAS BEEN TOLD THEE, O MAN . . ." The smell of the felt pen and its scratchy sound on cardboard fills me with longing for the classroom. Even Harry sensed my pleasure in being there, though I could not always wait out his storms.

". . . AND TO LOVE MERCY . . ." I print in silence. When I am done I move closer to my mother. "Do you remember the boy in London, the one in a wheelchair?"

"Teddy, wasn't it? With a padded helmet?" There is much my mother forgets these days, but not my stories.

"Just now, in California, I told some fourth graders about Teddy, and their reactions were interesting. They started off remembering the times they were not treated so well, but pretty soon they had their own stories of nice things that happened. Lucy described the way Marianne helped her learn English, so of course I told them your Masha story."

"Masha? Such a long time ago it was."

"But it was nearly the same story! Then Luis talked about his uncle who knows how sad he feels when he and his brothers fight, and Carmelita had a story about Jimmy who accidentally knocked her down and was so sorry afterwards he cried and gave her his dessert. And so then I told them about Harry."

"The fighter? The one in the blocks."

"Yes, that's Harry. I remembered a good story about him, when he was incredibly kind to an older boy who was being punished, someone he usually fought with. The thing is, with each story I could see that the children wanted to do something nice for someone, compliment them, or sit next to them. Some recognition of another person, a *connection* to another person had to be made."

My mother leans back and lifts her head, as if trying to discern a distant melody. "But don't you know, Vivian? The Hasidim did that in the old country! They taught people to think about goodness by telling them stories of holy men performing mitzvot, good deeds."

The connection between what I've been telling my mother and the religious sect of Jewish mystics called Hasidim astonishes me, mainly because I'd actually thought of it myself earlier but dropped the notion as being too esoteric. Not so for my mother, however, who has keen memories of a Hasidic grandfather and feels a sense of ownership about these matters.

"My grandfather, you know, was a follower of the Stoliner rebbe, one of the great Hasids," she went on. "That would be your great-grandfather. He loved those Hasidic stories and told them to us whenever we visited him. He said they were like prayers. That was a confusing idea to me, but the stories made us happy, a good thing because our lives were not easy." She fingers the printed message from Micah. "I told you some of them when you were little. Some of his stories, remember?"

"The one about the rabbi who disappeared every night?"

My mother's eyes are dancing. "Yes, the rabbi didn't show up until morning prayers. And he refused to say where he'd been all night. But one night someone followed him and saw him bringing wood from the forest to warm the huts of helpless old people. He wore the tattered cape and hood of a simple woodcutter."

A fresh memory brings a smile from my mother. "Your Aunt Becky and I pretended to be the characters in that story. 'Oh, thank you, kind stranger. Tell me who you are.' I'd be the old sick person and that's what I'd say. Becky always made up a different answer, even a princess. She wouldn't say she was the rabbi."

"How is it you never told us that?" I ask.

"I don't know why I didn't talk more about those days. For some reason a lot of things are coming back to me about my grandfather." Her eyes are wet. We have become too sad; this is not what I wanted. "But you did tell me about Masha and I was glad I could tell the children about her."

My mother smiles, retrieving another memory. "I just thought of something else Masha did. There was an older boy on the playground who started calling me 'first-grade baby' because I stayed with the younger children. Masha told him, 'What do you mean? Yetta is the sewing teacher!' She made it up, of course, but he believed her. She was like that, she knew what to do if someone was in trouble."

The thought of my mother so vulnerable in a strange place is painful to contemplate. Yet even those who speak the language can feel awkward and alone, and ashamed of being so, until some quite ordinary person comes along and knows what to do. Was it not Harry, most unlikely savior, who delivered Martin up from despair?

Every day in my classroom I made up stories and retold the fairy tales and folk legends of many cultures. But the stories presently on my mind seem of another kind. I don't have a name for them. My mother's comparison to Hasidic storytelling is compelling but falls outside my frame of reference. "Secular" is the road sign I have followed, barring certain other pathways that have beckoned along the route.

Teddy surfaces again in a Chicago high-school English class. I have been asked to explain my use of a tape recorder and daily journal to help me write about life in a classroom. The students are African American and Latino and I feel very Anglo standing in front of them.

A young man named Paul has been observing me closely throughout my recitation, but when I ask him, "Do you think it's important, in school, to tell and record stories such as the one I've just told about Teddy?" he looks away as if distrusting my question.

I am not discouraged. My question is vague, perhaps unanswerable. "You see, I've been traveling around lately talking to teachers and visiting classrooms. Let's say I describe my work as a writer, as I have today. Some students are involved, but others, their minds are elsewhere. However, if I use a story such as Teddy's as an example of what I enjoy writing about, something else happens. People will smile at each other, maybe tell a story of their own or talk about their feelings, as Luis and Lucy did. And soon the stories are connecting and lead us along other passages. So I wonder, what's this all about?" My question is directed to the whole class.

There is still no response but it is not an uncomfortable silence. Then Paul clears his throat and speaks. "See, we're used to so much shit, excuse me, garbage. We're always thinking about bad stuff. This Teddy kid and those others just seem to be, like, well, let's put it this way: while you were telling us those stories, I kept trying to remember if that's how I used to be, so nice and all. I recalled a couple things, and it made me feel, like, well, more relaxed, you could say."

Stanley, directly behind Paul, has been tapping on his desk with a pencil. "That don't change a thing, man," he says. "You get right back to being angry soon enough."

Tovah, her head piled high with beaded braids, raises her hand. "Yeah, sometimes it does, Stanley. Remember that lady gorilla, the one that saved the little boy?" Immediately everyone is nodding and grinning, including Stanley.

We are all familiar with the female gorilla at the Brookfield Zoo that rescued a toddler who toppled into her compound. She cradled and protected him from the other gorillas, then handed him over to a zoo-keeper. The story was on the front page of the local paper for a week. And now Tovah has only to mention the event to put everyone in a good mood.

"Binta Jua," comes a deep voice from the rear. "That's her name, Tovah."

She swivels around and smiles at the dreadlocked six-foot student who has remembered the gorilla's name. Then she looks at Mr. Flambeau, the teacher. "Listen to this," she says, an urgent quality in her voice.

"I'm on a bus going downtown to work. It's summer and it's hot and I'm in a mean mood. Mean! I hate those buses, so crowded and people being nasty and all, acting like you're a nobody. I don't ever want to give my seat to anyone and have to stand up and get pushed on. Well, anyway, some white guy yells out, 'Hey, guess what this gorilla did?' And he starts reading from the paper in a really loud voice. It's a big headline and all. A lot of people, like me, we're hearing it for the first time, you know?"

She glances my way, then sweeps the room, as if to make sure she has everyone's attention. "All of a sudden people are smiling and talking to each other, almost like friends. I never once saw that on a bus, early in the morning, everyone going to work—strangers to do that. Then someone asks this guy to read it again and some other people *they* start reading it and everybody is talking about the same thing and looking straight at each other. Here's what I mean. We're so *happy*."

I daydream. Does Tovah know that her name in Hebrew means "good"? Perhaps someone in her family is Jewish. To think about this right now is so irrelevant I almost laugh out loud.

Suddenly Tovah is on her feet twirling about. "Then

guess what I did! I got up and gave my seat to an old lady. I just up and did it. Without hardly knowing I was going to."

We stare at Tovah, our eyes growing larger along with hers. She lifts her arms above her head, encompassing us all in her joyful feeling. I see a Hasid dancing in a long black coat and fur hat. Stanley gives a resounding series of claps and one by one the class joins in his contagious rhythms.

Mr. Flambeau walks over to Tovah and the room becomes quiet. "Why did you decide to do that, Tovah?" he asks gently. "Tell us why you did that."

"Because, see, like everybody is loving that gorilla and I wanted to do something good too. I mean, I think that's why. I never even told anyone about it till now."

A shiver of recognition passes through the class; the students look at Mr. Flambeau, waiting for his comments. But he continues to watch Tovah. Then Thomas, in the front row, says, "People do come from gorillas, you know. Like a million years ago? We're sort of in the same family. 'Course most people they'll pass right by someone getting beat up, even if it's a kid." Thomas looks as if he might wish to elaborate but the bell rings and he is first to jump up. A few students stop to say goodbye; I long to convey my feelings but a simple thank you is all I can manage.

In the now empty room, Mr. Flambeau pours two mugs of dark steaming coffee from his thermos and opens a small tin of cookies. "I'd call what just happened to Tovah a spiritual experience," he says quietly. "*Two* such experiences: one on the bus and again in the classroom."

Sipping the sweetened brew, I weigh his unexpected declaration. "You are a religious man, Jerry," I say finally. "Most public school people don't refer to spiritual experiences."

"I'm the pastor of a church not far from here," he says, "and I guess it does color the way I view things. I've always been saddened by the absence of spirituality in school. No, the *potential* is here, wherever there are children, but we avoid the subject." He smiles at me. "You avoid it yourself, Vivian, in your books. To me, they're all about spirituality, but you never say so."

The context of our conversation has changed. I am not quite at home with Jerry's image of me. Was the Teddy incident a spiritual event or simply a deeply moving *human* event? Were all the times I have recognized a "moment of truth"—those glimpses into the nature of human expectations that so astonished me—

were they, in fact, religious experiences? Jerry Flambeau has a substantially different set of goals, it suddenly appears, and I must keep a measure of distance. Yet his certainty is appealing, even comforting.

"Jerry, I can see there is value in telling one another stories of these spontaneous acts of goodness. Tovah may even have been influenced by the Teddy story, or Luis's description of his uncle."

"We become witnesses," Jerry states. "We see who we are teaching, and we see who we are playing with, we see who we all might be."

I follow him to the sink, watching the soapy water pour over the mugs. "But, for you," I want to know, "what *is* the spiritual event? Is it the act itself, the story told about the act, the response of the listener?"

"All of the above." As he composes himself to speak, I see the Reverend Flambeau in his robes, a man of God. "At each point someone's suffering is understood by a larger and larger audience. To me the entire process is proof of the presence of God." He pauses to put the cups away and rinse the thermos. "But I have no objection if God is not mentioned. We can see in these events a victory for goodness, for connectedness to other people. We gain a new perspective on the struggle to overcome loneliness."

I have to interrupt. "Yes, loneliness, the major struggle when children enter school. And so the children pass along their stories to each other and somehow the terror subsides."

"Yes, yes!" Jerry sings out. "And now you are passing along the stories, and the stories, in and of themselves, lift our spirits. When we repeat them it is almost as if we are praying."

He does not notice my sudden intake of air. I am about to say that the Hasidim have the same idea, but he looks up at the clock and I know it is time for the next class to begin.

"My uncle told me about your visit," says an unfamiliar voice on the telephone. "I'm Rosalyn Flambeau. I teach kindergarten." She names a school in a lower income neighborhood on Chicago's West Side.

"He's a remarkable man, your uncle," I tell my caller. "I can't stop thinking about my conversation with him."

Rosalyn laughs. "Jerry has that effect on people. The reason I'm calling is to ask if I can visit your classroom. We read one of your books for an in-service and, if it's okay, I'd like to watch the storytelling and acting." She is disappointed to learn I no longer have a classroom.

"But I could come to yours, Rosalyn," I suggest. There is a pause, long enough to make me add, "Or you could come to my house, if you'd rather." But Rosalyn has already decided to invite me.

"Can you be at my school at seven?" she asks. "My kids need some explaining, a few of them do, that is. They're not easy this year."

When I arrive, we sit at a small table in her library corner. The walls of the classroom are covered with artwork, everything made by young hands. So great a sense of fantasy infuses the room, I am startled by Rosalyn's troubled confession. "I'm thinking about quitting," she says. "I haven't told my uncle, but he knows how frustrated I am much of the time."

My sympathy goes out to this intense young woman. "I've been there," I tell her. "There were times when I wanted to quit. But, in the end, I could never imagine myself in another place."

My counter-confession interests her. "Was it the children's behavior? It's the fighting that's gotten to me. It's never been this bad. I'm angry too much of the time and that doesn't help. There are five boys I cannot reach. Look at our lovely housekeeping area, and the blocks. I've had to close those off twice, there was so much fighting and destructiveness going on."

Five who fight is a large number. What would I have done with five Harrys? How could five Rudys be given "private time" in Miss Eliot's class? "Is it real fighting, Rosalyn?"

"Yes, serious stuff. No pretend about it. To me a fight is more than one hit, it's an exchange of blows. An attempt to hurt someone." Rosalyn's face reflects the pain she describes, but she goes on. "It starts mostly with verbal insults, name calling, teasing, but if it involves the word 'mother,' it escalates quickly. A mere mention does it and, being five-year-olds, they carry this to ridiculous extremes. William came crying to me yesterday. 'He's talking about my mom!' 'What did he say?' 'He saw her in the store!' That was all. And it was worth a fight. There is such an expectation of an insult no one listens to what's actually being said. The need to fight is taken for granted."

Rosalyn is not asking me for advice; she wants to present an accurate picture to someone she suspects is not intimately familiar with her situation. It is true that the fighting I've encountered is on a smaller scale. "In my class," I say, "the fights tended to be about space and materials, though I've had a few fighters of the sort you describe. Your combat does sound more intense and widespread, Rosalyn."

"Much more. I've been in schools like yours. Oh, sure, my kids will fight over a toy, or somebody knocks into something, but everything is taken as an intentional slight, an aggressive act; there's no middle ground." She takes a deep breath and a faint smile appears. "Don't be misled by my present mood. These are really loving and affectionate children. I love them dearly. The kids in the white school where I began teaching were distant and unresponsive by comparison. I'd much rather be here. But, it's the raw emotion that . . ."

There is a tapping on the door and Rosalyn calls out, "Come in, Esther! This is my friend, Esther Bonner, our other kindergarten teacher. I've asked her to join us because she's having a much better year. She'll give you a rosier picture than I can right now."

Esther is older than Rosalyn by at least twenty years. Both women are African American; it is clear they have established a strong friendship. "Rosalyn is having a rough year," Esther says. "I know she's been telling you about it. What she doesn't tell you is what a wonderful teacher she is! I keep wanting her to be sterner, more demanding, but she's not inclined that way, are you, honey?"

Rosalyn gazes warmly at her colleague. "I guess not. I just can't keep reacting in a punitive way, and I *have* tried. But I want the children to respond to my normal level of—what shall I call it? Polite persuasion? The boys I've mentioned won't listen unless I move toward them in a threatening manner. I have to sustain a level of anger that wears me out. Esther, I don't have my sense of humor anymore, the way you do. We hear your wonderful laugh all across the hall!"

"Well, I *do* have an easier group. But you have a whole bunch who are really doing well." Esther turns to me. "Rosalyn has some boys who belong in the Book of Job. They need psychological help, but it takes time to do these things and to help the family understand. Kids like this, when they get out of control, all we can do is send them to the office until a family member picks them up, hardly a good solution for a five-year old."

Rosalyn frowns. "You're better with those kids, Esther. You just seem to . . ."

"Now, I don't know about that. I've got a different style, I guess, a bit more—you know, we've talked so much about these things, wonderful talks. Actually, we're moving closer to each other's style. Rosalyn's gone to Yale, did she tell you? She's got some great ideas."

Rosalyn smiles shyly but her spirits have risen. "I agree, we're not that far apart," she admits. "We both want to be nice to the children and set good examples of kind and considerate behavior. But Esther is more traditional. She's less likely to choose play over paper work and table activities. She wants a minimum of distractions and I'm always going off on a tangent, it seems."

I laugh. "I'm that way myself, you know."

Esther nods vigorously. "Exactly! Rosalyn loves the things *you* love, Vivian. I say this from reading two of your books. The play and the stories. And, of course, the dramatics. But especially all that talk! I do admire that approach, I really do. I can see it makes for lively minds, and I want to adapt some of it to my program. But frankly, I worry that it will interfere with the structure I am building."

"Esther, tell the truth. You think I'm too wishy-washy," Rosalyn says. "But when Julian takes these five out of the room I can read one book after another and the children are ready to act them out and talk about them."

"She's terrific at discussions," Esther says proudly, but Rosalyn protests. "*Only* when someone removes Damone, Albert, and William. Yes, it's really those three. When they're not around, the other two do fine." She stops abruptly and slaps the table. "Okay! No more of this complaining! I've used up my quota for the week. By the way, my uncle said I should get you to tell your Teddy story. Do you mind? We've got time before the children come."

As I rush through the preliminary details, I realize I have two ways of telling the story, a shorter and longer form. It hasn't become ritualized, but I tend to add on the most recent responses. In this case it is Tovah's lady gorilla and the bus ride. When there is more time I include more of these reactions, as if the original story is not complete until I have demonstrated its effect on a variety of people. Even now I reach for my tape recorder, having forewarned both teachers I might want to tape parts of our conversation. "It's a long-standing habit," I offer as an excuse, and there are no objections.

I have barely finished the Teddy story before Rosalyn puts her hand on my arm. "Vivian, I have a wonderful example of that sort of thing. Would you like to hear it?" In her excitement she looks like one of the teenagers in her uncle's class. "It happened last week and I was so happy for a moment. Then I let myself forget it and sink into gloom again. Well, anyway, we were on our way to the gym. It's a long walk for my children. I always tell them, I know it's hard, but we need to be quiet in the hallway. As usual, the same five ran ahead, yelling. I warned them and threatened them but they kept on running, smacking into each other, moments away from a fight.

"When we got to the gym I was boiling mad. I just had to do something mean. So I kept the five boys outside in the hall. I told them, think of one thing you can do next time to keep from running, and I'll let you go in. Now, these boys *need* gym, they *love* gym, I wanted them to open that door and do some appropriate running, but I had to make my point!"

Rosalyn shakes her head sorrowfully. "I know, I know, it was a pointless response I was demanding from them, but I simply had to dominate, do you see? Albert, the weakest of the lot, could not handle the pressure. I saw right away this was a mistake. The others quickly made up some sort of answer, but Albert started going into a spin, a dangerous business, shaking his head and moaning. I was scared. I began looking around for help but the hallway was deserted."

Esther and I are on the edge of our chairs, the suspense almost too great. I want Rosalyn to speak faster and, reading my mind, she does. "Damone is pushing his way into the gym with the others when suddenly he catches a glimpse of Albert whose groaning and trembling has begun to escalate. In a flash, Damone is at his side, pressing into him, whispering softly. By the way, I can't tell you how often Damone is punched and kicked by Albert, a much larger child."

Rosalyn hunches over, as if she is Damone, murmuring into Albert's ear. "'Hey, man, my brother, watch me, sh-sh-sh, do what I'm showing you. Albert, my man, come on, you can do it, sh-sh-sh, do what I'm showing you, watch me, sh-sh-sh.' Albert keeps jerking around but Damone won't move an inch. He puts a finger on Albert's lips. 'Hey, man, keep cool, sh-sh-sh, do this, it's a good thing, she'll let you go in, sh-sh-sh-sh. Be my brother, man, do it, do it, do it.'"

I can barely breathe. Then Rosalyn sits up straight, raising her arms as Tovah did, her face beaming. "Albert quiets himself, staring at Damone with every ounce of his concentration. And then, miracle of miracles, he allows Damone to rescue him. He puffs out like a steam engine, 'Sh-sh-sh.'" Damone grabs Albert and hugs him—Albert, the boy who won't be touched! And off they go, into the gym, hand in hand."

Esther and I clasp hands and burst out laughing. We can't seem to take it all in. "Wow!" we finally explode in unison. I hear Rosalyn's uncle: "Yes, a spiritual moment. We are witnesses."

Rosalyn's children seem subdued. They may be intimidated by the presence of a stranger or by the fact that Damone's mother is seated against the wall. She has offered to stay because a day earlier her son had a difficult time and she had to be called.

After hanging up their jackets and backpacks the children go directly to their places at the large tables. The letter of the day, B, awaits them on individual work sheets, preparation for a group phonics lesson later in the morning. While the children begin to print rows of B's, Rosalyn and her assistant, Ron, move from child to child, speaking softly to each one. They point to the pictures in the margins—a baby, ball, bear, bunny, and bulldozer—making pleasant conversation with small groups. B-sounds bounce and bubble about the room, creating a gentle syncopation.

The mood is about to change. "Call that a B? That ain't no B!" Ron moves fast, placing a firm hand on William as Rosalyn rings a small bell. "Crayons down, please," she calls out brightly. "Mrs. Paley can't stay long and she's going to show us something special she does in her kindergarten." The crisis averted, Rosalyn moves us to the rug.

I take a roll of masking tape from my bag and set about to make a large rectangle, a foot or so inside the edge of the rug. "This will be our stage," I tell the children as I tear off pieces of tape. "Be careful of the tape, please. We'll need this stage to act our stories." A dozen little hands have already begun to finger the tape.

"First, let me repeat something Miss Flambeau told me about Damone and Albert." The children sit up straight, looking back and forth between the boys and me. "It's such a nice story, I must tell everyone."

All hands have left the tape; every face is turned to mine. "One day, on the way to gym, Albert, Damone, and a few others were running in the hall, making too much noise. Miss Flambeau decided to keep them out of the gym until each boy told her what he would do the next time, instead of running and shouting. Well, three boys figured out a good thing to say right away and went into the gym. Damone listened to the others and then figured out his good thing to say. He was about to go into the gym when he turned around and saw Albert. Poor Albert was all alone, having a terrible time. He just couldn't think of something to tell Miss Flambeau. Now, guess what Damone did?"

Everyone looks at Damone who seems to have forgotten what he did. His mother is equally curious and pulls her chair closer. I feel as if I am an actor on a stage before a spellbound audience. "Damone sat right down and gave Albert courage. 'Hey, man,' he said. 'Be my brother. Here's a good thing you can say. Sh-sh-sh! Say that. Sh-sh-sh, tell it to the teacher. Tell her you're going to say sh-sh-sh next time.'

"Well, now, imagine what Albert must have been thinking. 'Damone is my friend! He wants me to be happy!' So Albert went up to Miss Flambeau and put his finger on his lips. Sh-sh-sh, he told her. Then both boys went into the gym and they had a fine time."

Damone looks uncertainly at his mother, but she smiles at him; only then does he grin at Albert, knowing they have done something to make his mother proud.

My own performance is not over. "You've heard the real story and now I'll make it into a pretend story about some teddy bears and their teacher, Lady Bear." The children, of course, have no problem following the simple transition to fantasy. They do it themselves continually when they play.

"One day," I begin, "Lady Bear took her class for a walk through the piney woods to Sugar Hill, their favorite place to play. 'Now, remember,' she told the little bears, 'walk quietly past the old oak tree. There are new baby birds in the robin's nest. We mustn't disturb them.'"

Under my direction, half-a-dozen children form a line of bears with Lady Bear at the front and Billy Bear and Jackie Bear racing ahead. "*Pretend* run!" I caution. "Because if you run off the rug, you're no longer inside the story."

Annette, who is Lady Bear, needs no script from me. She is stern and unforgiving. "Sit here until you tell me a good thing!" she orders. "I'll be good!" squeals Billy Bear, but Jackie, amazingly adept at feigning a tantrum, cries and rolls on the ground until Billy says, "Do the shush thing, sh-sh-sh. Look, teacher, he's doing it!" Whereupon Lady Bear, surrounded by waves of shushing from everyone on the rug, says, "Now you can play on Sugar Hill."

Even before the actors have returned to their places, Annette's hand is waving an inch from my face. "I got one, okay? Can I do a story now?"

Rosalyn and I exchange glances and she answers for me. "Mrs. Paley has time for one story. Then she has to leave. We'll do more stories later. Mrs. Paley, can you write down Annette's story now, since she's ready?

When you're done, we'll come back and act it out. Meanwhile," her voice fades to a whisper, "let's be quiet little teddy bears who color their B-for-bear pictures." Rosalyn enters the spirit of the event without missing a beat.

Nor does it take Annette more than a moment to begin her story. "There was a mother," she dictates, while we are still standing. "Mine's not a bear, okay?" We find paper and pencil and sit down at the library table. "She losted her baby. She looked every place. What are you looking for, your baby? Here's your baby. I've been playing with your baby 'cause that's my sister."

When her classmates return to the rug, Annette announces that she will be the big sister, LaTonya offers to be the mother, but nearly everyone else wants to be the baby. "Well, then," I decide, "whoever wishes to be Baby may curl up on the rug and Big Sister will find you." The scenes are played with great seriousness, a peaceable kingdom lost and found.

Damone is first to jump up. "Why are you leaving?" he asks me. "I might have a story."

"Miss Flambeau and Mr. Peters will do your stories," I tell Damone and the others. "But I must visit my mother now. She's expecting me. I'll tell her all about my visit to your class."

The children, their upturned faces in every shade of brown, wait for further explanation. "I'll tell her about the B's and I'll tell her about Damone being a friend to Albert and about Lady Bear and her class. Then, when we're having our lunch, I'll tell Annette's story of the big sister, the mother, and the lost baby."

Rosalyn hands me my coat and we hug goodbye. After so many stories we are friends. Driving to my mother's, I see with renewed clarity the power of this activity I have pursued for so many years, the dramatization of children's stories. Annette's story is accepted as a gift by her classmates, an opportunity for them to share her vision of sisterly love. But, beyond that, to give someone a role to play—a lost baby, the suffering mother, the virtuous sibling—is akin to offering new life to a wandering soul. If this feels like a spiritual moment, why not call it that?

🐾 My mother and I sit quietly for a while as I complete some of her bookkeeping chores. Then she says, "I have a new story for you. It's about someone who lives here."

"Someone I know?"

"You don't know her. Sarah Harris. She's just started to sit with me at dinner." My mother stops, wondering how to continue. "Look," she says, finally, "I have to tell you something. When I go to the dining room now I'm not an interesting companion anymore."

She shifts uncomfortably. Exposing her vulnerability has never been easy for my mother. "I can't communicate the way I used to. My hearing aids pick up too much noise from all sides and, besides, I can barely see the people across the table. So people leave me out of their conversations. I don't blame them. But I do feel invisible sometimes and—"

"Mom, it really would make sense to move in with us. We keep asking you."

"No, I like living alone. It suits me. Now, can I tell my story?" she grins and pats my arm. "Last week I was seriously considering having my meals here in the apartment when a woman who has never been at my table began to sit with me. In fact, she saves me a seat if she's there first."

My mother grows uncharacteristically excited as she speaks of her new table mate. "Sarah Harris is a popular woman, always surrounded by people. But she wants to sit with me. And what do we talk about? School! She was a schoolteacher and she tells school stories!"

"You have no trouble hearing her?"

"She speaks slowly and distinctly, the way you do. She was a special education teacher and she remembers every child she ever had. She knows I enjoy hearing about them."

"Excuse me, Mom, but how could she know that? I'm a bit confused."

I think my mother is delighted to have a story that confuses me. "It's all because of your Teddy! One day Sarah Harris and two guests of hers sat at my table. I was alone. They were talking about someone they know who is now in a wheelchair and is very depressed. Not because she can't walk but because of the way people treat her, like a person who can't *talk*, a sick person. None of which she is."

"So you told them about Teddy."

"I told Sarah, really. She was the only one I could hear. I wanted her friend to know about Teddy. I'm not in a wheelchair, thank God, but I can imagine. Anyway, Sarah thought it was a beautiful story."

"You must have told it well, Mom. And now Sarah Harris is your friend."

"We talk together. Of course, she is an educated woman and I've had only two years of high school. But we tell each other stories." Her voice trails off.

I stir another cup of instant coffee for myself and

add hot water to my mother's tea. "Mom, I have an odd question for you. Have you ever witnessed a spiritual event?"

"Something to do with God? A miracle, do you mean? I don't know. Nowadays it's a miracle if people are just nice to each other."

"More than before?"

"No, before too. But I'm not sure about spiritual. You're asking the wrong person. I grew up in an observant home, but we didn't call things spiritual. Ma never told us God was watching us or even that God wanted us to do something. No, what she did was talk about 'mitzvot', good deeds. 'You earned a mitzvah,' she'd say, when I was especially nice to your Aunt Becky. You were supposed to always be trying to earn a mitzvah."

"We heard that often enough from you," I say, laughing.

"I got it from her, a habit. There was a girl in our building I didn't like, I can't remember why. Every day after school she'd knock on our door. 'Can Yetta play with me?' Ma never interfered with my social life. She was too busy for that. Sewing, you know, piece-work, so we could have food on the table. Anyway, whenever I said yes to this girl, Ma would whisper to me, 'Du hust fahrdin't ah mitzvah.' You earned a mitzvah."

"Did you ever ask Ma why a person is said to *earn* a mitzvah?"

"Well, don't forget we spoke Yiddish at home. So I was always translating from one language to another. But I think you have to *earn* the right to be called a good person. That was, to Ma, the whole idea, to be a good person."

"So, is Sarah Harris earning a mitzvah?" Without waiting for an answer, I ask another question. "What sort of stories does she tell you?"

"The kind you do, only most of her students had more serious problems. Yesterday she told me about a boy who kept repeating things, over and over. He'd knock on the door six times and wash his hands six times and hit a chair six times. The other children would help him count and remind him if he did it out of order. It had to done, you see, in the same order each time. After a while, he might say, 'I'm not doing that one anymore,' and the children remembered. It's amazing, isn't it? These children had their own problems but they watched *him* and helped him do the strange things he did. Simply because it was important to him."

I lean over and hug my mother. "See, it's happening again. Sarah told you this wonderful story and you're telling it to me. Now I'll repeat it to someone else.

Which part is the mitzvah? The original story or the retelling of it? I mean, Tovah needed us in order to tell her story; without us, the act of giving her bus seat to an old person was not complete. The same is true of Damone and Albert. Rosalyn tells me their story, I retell it to the children in several ways, and then to you. Maybe you'll pass it along to Sarah and it would remind her of another story."

"By the way," my mother says. "We don't only tell each other happy stories. Yesterday she asked me what my earliest memory was. We were talking about a sadness in her family and I remembered something that happened when I was two. We were living for a while with my grandfather, in Visotzk, a shtetl. Our own village, Gideen, was just a dorph. It had almost no Jews, so on holidays we went to our grandfather's house."

"The one who followed the Stoliner rebbe?"

"Yes, the one who told us stories. But this earliest memory of mine was very scary; even when I told Sarah it was scary. It was nighttime and someone set our house on fire. We were huddled together in my grandfather's cart and his old horse was pulling us away. I turned around and saw the house, a small wooden house, outlined inside the flames, and I cried out to Ma, 'Am I still inside my zeide's house?'"

"How awful! Who burned down the house?"

"I don't know. Nobody ever talked about it. But I got the impression somebody did it, that it was not an accident."

"You never told me that story, Mom. You hardly ever told us how it was in the old country. Dad didn't either. There you are, a little child, watching your grandfather's house burn and trying to figure out if you are still inside. What a story!"

"Better not to dwell on it," my mother cautions. "My Masha story made you happy. This one makes you sad."

"I know. But this story is as important as the Masha story. Remember Luis, the fourth grader from California? He kept asking me, don't I know any mean stories?"

"You wouldn't have told him this one."

"Probably not. But that might be more my problem than his."

Suddenly I remember a nightmare Harry once told us at lunch. In shuddering detail he described his mother being dragged screaming from his side by bearded robbers in a long car, speeding away, with no one there to see what happened. I thought at the time it was the most frightening nightmare I'd ever heard from a child.

The next day Sheila, a shy girl who barely ever spoke

to Harry, dictated her own dream as a story to be acted out. She was in a secret garden with beautiful roses all around and lilies on a pond. One sentence in her story became our mantra for a while: "It was always peaceful and there was never any fighting."

Harry listened to Sheila's story three times: as I wrote it down, while we acted it out, and, finally, a few days later, when he asked Sheila to bring it to me to read again. I wondered about the two dreams: Did the "good" dream make sense to Harry because he had told us his nightmare? Did Sheila retrieve her idyllic vision to ward off the effects of Harry's awful scene? Even now, the mysterious connection eludes me. But thereafter, when Harry would see Sheila crayoning alone at a table, he'd leave the blocks and sit beside her, drawing his graceful animals that seemed to be flying.

I blunder seriously at my next conference where I am to speak about such matters as tolerance and inclusion. An event takes place that shakes my confidence and leaves me disheartened and ashamed.

As I spin out my web of stories, from Teddy to Sarah Harris, the structure feels large enough to contain everyone. It does not occur to me that this new role I've given myself proceeds too smoothly. No longer am I tested each day as I was in the classroom. *There* it was quite impossible to cover my mistakes; here, upon this podium, the illusion of virtue comes easily. Not today, however.

During the discussion that follows my talk, individual voices of conference participants begin to emerge. I am reminded of the fourth graders in the California school; these adults also, it seems, must first reveal their reasons for sadness before they can remember why they are hopeful.

One African American woman recalls her sense of shame when white college dormitory mates complain about her hair straightening process, unfamiliar and unappealing to them. "Why can't she do that smelly thing in a beauty parlor?" they demand. To explain her inability to pay for professional services would be further humiliation and so the conflict blighted her college days.

Later, teaching sixth grade in a rural area, she thought she could begin finally to tell some of the pieces of her story. It was important, for example, to explain to white colleagues how destructive it is to call a black male student "boy". When they yelled out, "Get in line, boy!" she could feel the young man's anger.

However, once again *her* life experience was discounted as trivial and irrelevant.

In quick order come other stories of harm done in the name of conformity or ignorance to those silenced in school: a stutterer, a Native American woman whose clothing is disparaged, a man rejected and teased for his awkwardness on the playing field, a woman for being overweight. There seem to be no "good" stories to balance the scale. It must be easier for children, in their eagerness to find evidence of love and acceptance, to slough off the bad stuff. Children, luckily, can still imagine themselves in heroic roles.

The people in my audience are not children; they are the men and women who teach the children. I long for someone to give me a *good* story but none are forthcoming. Memories of injustices are so sharply etched they overwhelm me, yet I can no longer concentrate on their separate contours. I find myself wishing I were in a classroom of children, lifted out of despair by puppies running about in the sunshine and big sisters playing with lost babies.

A solemn, mustached man is speaking. He describes a childhood event in which he is repeatedly excluded from gym teams because he is Mexican. "Don't pick that . . ." the boys shout, but I cannot make out the epithet. I frown and shake my head sympathetically, then turn to someone on the other side of the room.

Suddenly, a young blond woman stands and begins to berate me. "You didn't listen to him!" she shouts. "To the Mexican guy! None of us listened. He was telling us something, that he was treated like dirt, and you didn't stay with him, you left him hanging!"

I feel faint, as if I need air. "My name is Madeleine," she continues, "but you didn't find out *his* name—or what they called him, the bad words, so we would know what they are!" She is sobbing as she moves toward me. "We listened to your stories but you practically ignored him." She stops to wipe her eyes, then says in a lower voice, "In your books you don't ignore a single child's story."

The audience is stunned. People avoid each other's gaze but I cannot take my eyes away from the woman. "Thank you, Madeleine. You are right, of course." I turn to the man. "I'm sorry, I don't know your name."

He rises slowly, gripping the arms of the chair. "My name is Manny. Listen, it's okay. You're up there and so many people wanted to speak."

"No, Manny, I truly am sorry, deeply sorry. It wasn't okay. You revealed a painful memory. That was a good deed. My mother, if she were here, would have understood better than I that you were showing us how to become good people. Madeleine understood that."

An elderly man in the audience stands. "Manny, what should all of us have said to you?"

Manny is surprised by the question. "I guess I wanted people to say, 'That was a bad thing they did. You didn't deserve it.'" He waves to Madeleine. "That lady there is braver than I am. My daughter is like that too, but I've been silent too long."

Someone claps and others follow suit, releasing us from tension. The meeting has ended. Immediately, there is a crowd around Manny and another surrounding Madeleine. Several people line up to speak to me or bring me books to sign but my usual pleasure in this is not there. I would prefer to be alone.

"This is pretty dramatic stuff," a black man says to me. "When that woman cried, I remembered a few times, even when I was a kid, that I should have defended someone, but I didn't speak up. Even now, in a faculty room, I don't. She did a good thing. No one here will forget it soon."

Yes, Madeleine did a good thing. She recognized another person's suffering and was moved to do something. But why hadn't I? Luis had warned me: "Sometimes people isn't that nice," he had said. "They move away in the middle of what I try to tell them. Even I had a teacher to do this."

Flying home, I find a measure of comfort by writing in my journal: "What happened there? I begin by telling stories in which acts of goodness are revealed. Then *they* tell stories in which *badness* is the point. Yet all their stories add up to one woman doing a good thing, a mitzvah. It has turned out after all to be a good story, except that I am not the hero. This hurts. Like Tovah, I want to be the hero. But I neglected to stand up and give someone my seat."

My mother listens to my repentant tale without comment. Her apartment has suddenly become dark, a storm approaching over the lake. She turns on the table lamp and begins leafing through her Rabbi Hertz edition of the Torah while I switch on the other lights. Neither of us likes a dark room.

"I'm looking for something, Vivian, somewhere at the end of Deuteronomy," she says, peering through the small lens in her hand. I'm always amazed at her dexterity with this awkward tool. "What you said before, about it being too hard to listen to everyone, that it would take a saint, reminds me of something in the

Torah. Would you like to make some coffee? This may take me a while to find."

I busy myself in her little kitchen, straightening the pill bottles and putting away dishes while I wait for the kettle to whistle. But before the first wisp of steam, my mother calls out, "Look here! There's even a mark on the page. Who knows how long ago I made it."

Leaning over the table, I read aloud from Chapter 30, verse 11: "For this commandment which I command this day, it is not too hard for thee, neither is it far off." A pencilled arrow, entered by my mother at a time when she too needed to study these words, urges me on to verses 12, 13, and 14.

"It is not in heaven that thou shouldest say, 'Who shall go up to heaven, and bring it to us, and make us to hear it, that we may do it?' Neither is it beyond the sea, that thou shouldest say, 'Who shall go over the sea for us and make us to hear it that we may do it?' But the word is very nigh unto thee, in thy mouth, and in thy heart, that thou mayest do it."

At the bottom of the page are the various rabbinic interpretations, a running commentary I have always found essential to my understanding of most biblical passages. But this explanation of what I have just read seems written for me alone.

"It is not too hard," the reader is told, "nor too distant: but nigh, clear and practicable . . . it is not out of reach, out of ken, far removed from the sphere of ordinary life . . . It is not something inaccessible or supernatural, making it necessary for a person to scale the heights of heaven to find it and bring it down to earth!"

I take a cardboard strip and felt pen from the drawer and copy, in large print, "IT IS NOT IN HEAVEN." This quotation will go on my desk, not my mother's, to remind me that the task of listening to every voice is not for saints alone; it is not too hard for ordinary people, in ordinary places. What is more ordinary than a classroom?

Looking up, I see that my mother dozes in her chair. I turn off the whistling kettle, then read further in Deuteronomy. I am immediately caught up in the expression "little ones" in Chapter 31, verse 12. "Assemble the people, the men and women and the little ones . . . that they may hear and they may learn." Little ones? I cannot recall seeing "little ones" before in the Torah and am pleased to note it will be explained below in the commentary.

"None realized more clearly than the Rabbis," says the footnote, "the spiritual power that comes from the mouths of babes and sucklings. 'The moral universe rests upon the breath of schoolchildren' is one of their deep sayings."

The power of this statement overwhelms me. The moral universe rests upon the breath of schoolchildren? Of course, this could be interpreted as resting upon what we teach children when they are young. But I prefer to think it refers to what the children already know and can teach us.

If the moral universe takes its shape in the words of the young, then my passion for listening to their words has not been excessive. I think in fact, I have not gone far enough; more is revealed by children than I have recorded.

My mother opens her eyes. "Did I sleep long?" she asks.

"Ten minutes, maybe. But listen to what I found here. A rabbi said this long ago. 'The moral universe rests upon the breath of schoolchildren.' How is it I never came across this before? Do you remember reading it?" I repeat the passage slowly, then the two of us sit together in silence, watching the freezing rain beat on the windows. By the time I leave it will have turned to a gentle snow, but for now the fierceness of the storm matches the explosive force of the words we have discovered in the Torah.

Cass and I are back on the beach. Everywhere is the stillness of deep snow, pure white, but for the occasional footprints of deer and a few hardy seagulls. The wind off the lake keeps a narrow path open for our sunrise hike and a frozen rosy glow in the sky begins to light the way.

The color display is astonishing, yet it is Manny I see. He stands there, arms out, trying to explain his childhood humiliations. If only I could step back into that scene; this time I would not look away. It was Manny's turn to be listened to and I failed him. What if the classroom is the only place left where we are guaranteed a full turn on the stage? If people move away and do not listen we may forever feel disconnected. Madeleine knew the feeling and cried out in protest.

There is an ancient wisdom hidden here. A teacher once told a group I was part of that when a member of the San people of southern Africa is away from the tribe for even a day, he is said to have died. "Since I cannot hear the stories told when I am gone," a man explained to her, "then I have died on that day."

The speaker was deeply moved by what the man said. "You see, each one must tell his own story," she continued. "No one can speak for another person. Outsiders don't even know the true name of the San. They call them Bushmen, which is not what they call themselves. So how could anyone else tell their story?"

The imagery of isolation invoked by the San story had a profound effect on the audience. I thought of Martin, sent away from his classmates. He must surely have known the feelings of the San people as he sat alone in the hallway. He was deprived of every story revealed to others and he could not tell his own. Even when a child returns to school after being away, the only story recounted will be the teacher's, which is to say, the math or science facts that may have been missed during the absence. No one will retrieve what was said by the other children in the class. Yet it is this information the child most yearns to hear. Harry understood Martin's loss, compensating him with cookies.

My own awakening as a teacher came about through listening to the same stories the children want to hear. Their voices alone kept me from losing my way in the classroom. In order to capture more of what was being said, I allowed the children's play to continue and inevitably the play itself became a story that could be told again and again. "Remember when we played we were lost and a good witch came? Let's do that again."

I began to ask children to dictate these spontaneous

episodes to me so we could act them out for all to see and take part in, wanting to come closer to the meaning of each story. Why did the children take their play so seriously? What was it that produced such concentration and emotional commitment? Somewhere in this play lay deeper explanations than could be described by the grownups, who may have forgotten the questions.

If, for example, in the process of pretending to be someone or something else, children learn, even for a moment, to walk in another person's footsteps, could this be the supreme mitzvah of all?

Pretend you are a lost baby, a frantic mother, a heroic sister: feel the pain, celebrate the rescue. Pretend you are a gloriously playful puppy, knowing that the storyteller, moments earlier, would not let you play with him in the blocks; miraculously, he now revives your faith in him, in his potential as a friend.

If the need to know how someone else feels is the rock upon which the moral universe depends, then the ancient sages were right. For this is surely what happens when children give each other roles to play in their continual inquiry into the nature of human connections. It is as schoolchildren that we begin life's investigations of these weighty matters.

My mind races backwards. What of younger than school-age children? How early does this inclination to be a friend in need show itself? I recall two babies in a day care center playing out a wordless scene, unnoticed by their teachers. Peter, not more than eighteen months old, having placed a ball at the edge of a table, is surprised when the ball rolls off and comes to a stop at Thea's foot. In a crawling, partly walking maneuver, she returns the ball and stays to watch as Peter puts it back on the table. Again the ball rolls off.

Both children glance at their nearby teacher, busy rocking an infant and reading to a toddler. A frown spreads over Peter's face as he retrieves the ball from under a cabinet. Hesitantly he repositions it on the table but this time, as he removes his hand, a tiny arm shoots out to keep the ball in place. Thea has pulled herself up to full height to come to Peter's aid.

The children stare at each other and then Peter smiles. A great and mysterious event has taken place and neither child moves to alter the balance until a bell sounds announcing snack time. The magical moment is gone as the quickly forgotten ball bounces into another room.

At the snack table, Peter is unable to report Thea's

act of kindness but, somewhere, perhaps, the moral universe has taken notice.

Another scene comes to mind, not unlike the one in the day-care center. This time the girl and boy who rock the universe are fifth graders, seated with their class on the floor of an art museum. Everyone is staring at a neon tube structure that flashes streaks of reds and blues and yellows across the wall and on the face of the docent.

"What do you think the artist had in mind?" she asks the children. At first no one answers but then a boy offers a statement of fact. "This can't go in a house that don't have lights, you know." Before the docent can respond the teacher bends over and whispers, "Stop being silly, Dominick!" A few children giggle.

But not the girl next to him. Her name tag tells me she is Abby. While several of the other students attempt an answer to the docent's question, Abby speaks quietly to Dominick. "Do you mean, like if someone is poor and didn't pay the electric bill? So then that thing wouldn't work?"

Dominick nods gratefully. "Yeah. Or you could live on the top of a mountain," he says, "and there ain't even any wires going up there. So they can just have a *picture* of it, see, not this kind of thing." The teacher frowns at them and the two children stop talking. But they sit up straighter and each carries the look of a secret sharer.

Can Dominick and Abby possibly sense the importance of what has just taken place? Together they have created a moment of mutual respect and dignity that seems, in itself, a work of art. They are witnesses, Reverend Flambeau would say. "It's a spiritual experience."

In the spring, I meet Alain, a school director, at a conference in Luxembourg. He invites me to come home with him between sessions and we sit now in his garden where he questions me about certain aspects of American education. However, my attention has been captured by his two-year-old daughter, Marie, who plays beside a pond. Her intense preoccupation with something she sees in the grass seems to me a most wonderful thing; perhaps I have forgotten the natural tendency of a young child to study, with great concentration, that which interests her at the moment.

"Papa," she calls, pointing to a snail emerging from its shell, "can I have it?" She speaks in Letzebuergesch, a language I do not know, but I grasp her meaning for she acts out every thought. Her father fills in the missing words for me.

Alain drops the snail into Marie's hand. "Oh no!" she cries, letting it fall. She watches the snail move toward the water. "Papa, I want it!" comes her renewed demand.

Again, Alain gives the snail to his daughter; but once more she shrieks and drops it, puzzled at her own behavior. She wants to play with the snail yet is compelled to withdraw from the strange creature. "If the snail were a child," Alain comments, "Marie would know better what to do. She has only a few playmates but she can usually create a connection when she meets a child in the park."

Marie follows the snail to the edge of the pond and notices several other snails of various sizes. Her eyes grow large. "Papa, the mama snail! She wants her baby to play with me. Because he is lonely."

"Does the baby snail wish to play?" Alain asks.

"Yes, we are friends, in school." Alain places the smallest snail in Marie's basket. "Put Mama in too, and Papa, or Baby will cry." Humming softly, Marie comforts the snail family with leaves and grasses, then walks around slowly, swinging the basket. "Going to school, going to school," she sings in falsetto. "Push me, push me, on the swing." She sinks into the soft grass, cradling the basket. "Time to read," she trills, holding up her hands as if displaying a book, until her attention moves to an odd-shaped twig. Into the basket it goes and Marie's snail squeal informs us that it is meant to be an intruder of some kind, perhaps a snake. The drama continues, narrated too softly for us to hear. We can no longer spy on the moment of creation.

After Marie goes inside to nap, I compare her snail drama to Annette's lost baby story. "The two have much in common," I suggest.

"Though Marie's story occurs in a natural state," Alain replies, "and Annette's comes about in a kinder-garten storytelling activity. Yet it's true. Both girls create helpless characters and give them roles to play. All these things in Marie's story, by the way, have been on her mind. We're expecting a baby, you know, and we've begun to speak about school for Marie, after the baby comes. We think she'll need children to play with, but all of it worries her. Maybe your Annette is also worried about a new baby replacing her."

"Quite possibly," I say. "So first she imagines the baby gone and then she performs its safe rescue. But, Alain, I must ask why you think Marie's story takes place in a more natural state than Annette's? Telling your story to other children and having them play in it seems at least as natural if the intention of storytelling is to bring others into your world in this highly focused way."

Alain laughs. "I see what you mean. That reminds me of the old puzzle: if a tree falls in the forest and no one hears it, was there a sound? In other words, the stories no one hears or takes part in, have they been told? Have they fulfilled their function?"

A small kitten appears from behind the house and leaps into Alain's lap. "But are not these purposes profound?" he muses, rubbing the kitten's back. "One must be a philosopher. Have you read Gareth Matthews? He says the children are true philosophers, that they deal with exactly the same issues as adult philosophers."

He puts down the kitten and begins to gather the toys strewn about the lawn. "And what do the children philosophize about?" he continues. "How to gain access to every person, feeling, thing, and event. The computer cannot help them with this, I keep reminding the teachers in my school. For information, yes, but not reflection. Oh, by the way, our kindergarten teacher, Margot, who is, in fact, big on computers, also uses your storytelling and story acting. She would like you to watch. None of her children speak English but she and I will translate when necessary."

The next morning Alain brings me to Margot's room during free activity time. I begin watching a pair of puppet players, Sonia and Nina, recent immigrants from Portugal. Their enthusiasm attracts me, though I don't understand a word they are saying. Nor does Margot, I discover, for the girls are speaking Portuguese. As Margot attempts to find out what the puppet play is about, Nina nervously whispers her replies to Sonia, letting her friend act as translator. "Nina has not learned our language yet," Margot tells me.

The plot is a familiar one: two princesses are lost in a dark forest. My granddaughters' puppets also wandered in some unknown woods, looking for a rescuer or for someone to rescue; whatever the story required, their older brother would try to fill the role, just as now a boy named Paul will be summoned to do.

Paul looks a bit lost himself, a character in search of a story, it seems to me. "Paul, Paul, come here!" the girls call, and I wonder what language they are using. However, since Nina speaks directly to Paul, he too must be Portuguese. The girls push a rabbit puppet at him and tell him to hide behind the curtain. Moments later, pretending surprise, they pull him out. Paul's look of gratitude reminds me of Teddy's: each boy has been saved from obscurity.

Meanwhile Margot has been writing down children's stories at a small table in the center of the room, jumping up frequently to help one group or another, but remarkably steadfast in her goal of listening to each storyteller. Now, with half a dozen stories in hand, she calls the children to sit around a rug. Alain has returned to be my translator.

To our surprise, Nina's story will be first. But how could Margot have taken down her story? Did Sonia translate each sentence for her? Apparently the solution comes from Nina herself; she has used her mother as a scribe and brought two copies of a story to school, one in Portuguese and the other in Letzebuergesch.

Awkwardly, Margot attempts the first sentence in Portuguese and is about to follow up with its counterpart when an amazing thing happens. Nina strides into the center of the rug and speaks to her classmates in Letzebuergesch. Alain, himself puzzled, turns to me and whispers, "What's going on?"

Suddenly Nina needs no intermediary. She has stepped forward in full command of character, plot, and dialogue. Two sisters and two brothers go to the pet store to buy a puppy but return with a puppy and a kitten. "I told you *one* puppy!" their mother shouts. "But they are friends," the siblings explain, whereupon a proud mother orders them to feed their pets.

The entire production has been in Letzebuergesch under the confident direction of its author. She now returns to the outer edge of the rug, eyes lowered, whispering to Sonia in nervous imitation of a shy child.

At lunch, Margot, Alain, and I talk about the unusual event. "But why the charade?" Alain wonders. "Does she feel too much an outsider?"

Margot nods. "That must be it. Yet something in the story was urgent enough for her to drop the disguise."

"Yes, exactly!" In my excitement I nearly topple a tall glass of water in the path of my waving hand. "Tell me if you think I may be right. The story became Nina's conduit, just as Sonia has been. It serves the same purpose as a friend. With a friend, you can remove your disguise."

It is time to tell Margot and Alain about Teddy, for he too is in disguise. His condition prevents him from ordinary discourse with children, but when he enters play or a story, the real Teddy emerges. "If Teddy were in my class," I wonder aloud, "would I be able to help him tell his own story?"

"The children would find a way," Alain says, but the

remainder of his thought must wait, for a parent has stopped to speak to him, allowing me to pursue my own musings. Teddy's conduit had been both Edmond's story and the cash register exchange with the Indian boy. That dialogue contained but two statements, the name of a cereal from Teddy and the adult-sounding "Here you are, sir!" from the other child. Yet, an entire world of acceptance and belonging opened for the "stranger" and "homeborn" alike. "The stranger that sojourneth with you shall be unto you as the homeborn among you, and thou shalt love him as thyself." This passage from Leviticus is surely the forerunner of the one in Deuteronomy. "It is not in heaven . . . the word is very nigh unto thee, in thy mouth, and in thy heart, that thou mayest do it."

I feel myself smiling. Have I moved to a new place where scripture motivates the discourse? And yet, may I not quote from ancient writings without signifying religious intent? Even as I ask myself these questions, the answer is clear. Of course, I and everyone else may sing out such passages in the Bible that cause us to feel we have just seen the great blue heron take wing and soar above the tree tops. But my language will always, I think, be that of the secular classroom. Having said this, I wish I *were* more comfortable with those spiritual phrases used by the good Reverend Flambeau and by my own rabbi as well. Often, it sounds more convincing.

I am reminded of an incident in my visit to a Catholic school classroom. I was invited to carry on a discussion concerning my classroom rule, "You can't say you can't play." Since it became the title of a book I wrote, the idea had received a certain amount of extra attention.

The third graders in the discussion tried to imagine what it could mean, this notion of not rejecting a classmate. For some the plan was radical, even a bit threatening, until a boy came upon a new way of thinking about it.

"Why don't you tell everyone," he suggested, "that *God* says, 'You can't say you can't play.' Then no one will argue." I could see the smiles of recognition all over the room. Ah yes, the children must have felt, this would be a more sensible way to proceed.

In early June I come upon another Teddy story. By sheer luck or destiny I meet a schoolteacher named Minna walking along the beach wondering why she cannot get a certain boy off her mind. Furthermore, when she discovers that I too am a teacher she is compelled to put him into my mind. I know the feeling.

It is Cass, reminding her of her own Labrador retrievers, who brings us together, but when we discover we are both teachers the topic quickly switches to children. "This past year," Minna tells me, "I had a boy who entered my first grade as a truck. Wherever he went in that classroom he was driving a truck." She waits for my response before going on.

"I once had just such a boy," I say. "Jason was a helicopter."

We smile knowingly. "Timmy would be shifting gears, making the appropriate noises, doing the windshield wipers, in short, whatever a truck does he would do. And he remained a truck all through the year. No matter where he went, to the lunchroom, the gym, the library, he was a truck."

"How did the other children react?"

Minna laughs. "They'd be riding in the back of the truck as he went down the hallway. Not one child ever denied him his right to be a truck."

"Was it because *you* accepted him as a truck?" I suggest. "What if you had acted annoyed or impatient—or concerned?"

"I don't know," Minna replies, "but I remained constant. It wasn't hard at all. If I was holding his hand he would sometimes be pulling me all over the hallway, from side to side. When I questioned him, 'What are you doing, Timmy?' he'd say, 'I need an alignment, I can't keep this truck on the road.' I'd say, 'You're going to have to get that done, or you'll get a ticket. You can't drive like that!' This was the way we communicated, not all the time, but much of the time."

Minna throws a stick into the water for Cass to retrieve. He senses her confidence and drops the stick at her feet instead of mine. After two more tosses, Minna resumes her story.

"Another time, Timmy complained that he was sliding all over the road, pretending it was icy. 'I've got to throw on a set of chains!' he yells. And so, of course, we all must stop and wait while he adjusts his chains. You see, his truck was always breaking down. It needed work, all the time."

"This was true of my helicopter boy," I tell Minna. "The blades were continually breaking and needed to be fixed. Unwanted intrusions, in particular, always resulted in broken blades. Jason seemed to want to keep us away but, like Timmy and his broken truck, this passion for the helicopter organized us around him."

She points to the house, set off from the beach, where she is spending the weekend with cousins, but tells me nothing about them. It is Timmy we both want to discuss. "The breaking and fixing became a class ritual," Minna goes on. "And it wasn't only the truck. In the corner of my classroom we have a little recycling center. Timmy'd go back there and rummage around as if he were fixing a fire in the stove. In our rural area, if you work in your garage or shop you have to keep a fire alive in the stove to stay warm. Timmy was always doing something to keep the fire going, quite realistically, so he could work on his truck."

Minna explains that she lives in a small community on Lake Superior. "It's truly rural," she says. "We're mostly Lutheran, church-going people, originally from Finland. It used to be farm land but that became too poor for use. Now it's a case of finding work where we can, usually in other towns. My husband and I are teachers, so we're lucky. Being a schoolteacher is an extraordinarily good job up there. Many of our families barely make a living. The hunting and fishing help."

As she speaks I envision a community different from any I've known. And yet Timmy's story, like Teddy's, could take place anywhere that children come together. Does the moral universe rest upon the children's acceptance of Timmy's truck? "I'll bet your children are well informed about trucks," I say.

"There are trucks all over the place," she says, laughing, "and in constant need of repair, it seems. Our Timmy would not likely be a helicopter. You'd be amazed at how knowledgeably he drove his truck. When he backed up he shifted it in reverse; when he'd go forward he'd go through each of the three gears until he was in high."

"I'm curious, Minna. Did anyone else become a truck?"

"No, it never occurred to anyone. This was Timmy's role." She stoops to pick up a pebble, examines it and puts it in her pocket. "Did anyone in your room decide to be a helicopter?"

"As a matter of fact, no. Nor a vehicle of any kind. Maybe there is room for only one passion of this sort in a classroom. It comes of such deep motivation it cannot be copied."

"Or erased, apparently," she adds. "Not that the others didn't sometimes cause problems for Timmy, but they didn't spoil his illusion. I remember once Timmy came running to me, angry. 'See those guys over there? They just punctured all my tires! My tires are flat!' 'Why did they do that?' I asked. He couldn't figure it out, but soon the boys were calling him back. 'We've got 'em fixed. Come on! We'll put 'em back on!'"

I ask Minna if she thinks Timmy will still be a truck

in second grade. She too has wondered about this. "He wasn't one in kindergarten. He had a tough time there, actually. I'm told he was a fighter, that he hurt children. There was some doubt about sending him on to a regular first grade. But they let him try out my class and that seems to be when he decided to be a truck. Somehow it was the most natural thing in the world to him and to me. I never discussed this with anyone. Timmy would be a truck, that's all."

I feel the old excitement growing. "You knew he had to pretend he was a truck, that he needed the disguise. And the children knew it too. But if you had been a spoiler, they might not have felt free to enter Timmy's story."

Minna throws another stick for Cass, sneaking a sideways glance at me. Who is this grey-haired lady giving speeches on the beach? "Vivian, I'm wondering, are you something besides a schoolteacher?"

Her question strikes me as funny but I don't laugh. "You're not used to another teacher becoming so involved in a story you've told?"

"To tell the truth," Minna admits, "I'm not much accustomed to telling such stories. I haven't really talked about Timmy to anyone but the special ed teacher and it didn't seem so much like a story when I did. It was more like a list of problems, though we really didn't feel that way." She looks around for Cass who is chasing after a flock of gulls. "You might not believe it, but I'm usually a rather shy person. Here, on the beach, with a stranger, I've been talking up a storm. And, by the way, you didn't answer my question."

An accurate response might be, aren't we all something besides a schoolteacher? But this is not a time for verbal games. We've been entirely serious with one another, two strangers on the beach. "As it happens," I say, "I do write books about my classroom, stories about the children and their—"

Her face shines with recognition. "I *thought* your helicopter boy sounded familiar! It's on our recommended list for summer reading but . . ." She blushes. "I haven't read it yet."

"Don't worry, Minna. There are a dozen books on my list I haven't read yet."

She protests. "No, but I really do want to read that particular book, and I'll tell you why. It's described as being about the children's storytelling and about their dramatics. I'm curious about this. I think it could be something I have to know about. You see, when I was little I was painfully shy. But it was easier for me to speak to people if I had a role in a play. The trouble was, I was hardly ever picked, because I was so shy. It was very painful. I can never forget those feelings. Funny thing is, with all Timmy's intrusive truck behavior, I see him as the same shy person I was."

We have come to the end of the broad sandy beach. Before doubling back, we decide to sit for a while on a bench we see a few yards into the forest. The moment we're seated I launch into the Teddy story, as if it is the most natural topic in the world. I keep going, on to Damone and Albert, and finally bring in Harry. Sitting here with Minna, gazing out at the endless shades of blue where the water meets the sky, it seems that every story I know is connected to her boy who would be a truck.

Suddenly Minna says, "I wish you could visit my school. If we were closer to Chicago, it might be possible."

"It's still possible, you know. I'd like to come to the sort of rural school you describe, where children live outdoors so much of the time. I'm used to children who are more confined and go to after-school and even before-school programs."

Minna smiles. "You won't find a more rural place than ours. There's not even a hotel you could stay in, but I've got a comfortable guest room and we'd love to have you. Are you really interested in coming? It's a five-hour drive north from here—and, of course, twice that from Chicago."

"London is farther," I state simply. "And if I'm up here already? Yes, I would definitely like to come. Something tells me I should do this."

"Why?"

Her question is bold and direct, but I think I can answer, at least in part. "For one thing, I'd like to look at my storytelling and story acting with a new group of children, maybe even do this in first, second, and third grades, as well as kindergarten. If there's time. I want to watch it evolve across the grades. My own storytellers have been urban dwellers as you know, so here's a chance to see how it works in a rural school."

"Is the second thing Timmy?"

"Okay, he's on my mind too, I admit." We giggle like schoolgirls and begin our trek back on the beach. "Look, Minna, I feel the need to immerse myself in a school for more than a day. Maybe for a *week*. I'll walk into the children's lives, a stranger, unannounced and unexplained, asking the children for their stories so we can act them out. Such a request will be a novelty."

"Yes, completely. It's not done in our school."

"Good. Then we can all see what will happen. You

and the other teachers too, not just me. By the way, will they want me to come?"

"I'm sure they will. Do we say anything about Timmy?"

"No, nothing about Timmy and the truck. That's just between us." We walk along silently for a while and then I return to Timmy. "Maybe it *is* all about Timmy. The moment you told me about him I wanted to meet him. Here is a child who has spent an entire year living one story and bringing all of you into it, on his terms. When you think about it, he's provided a source of continuity for the entire class and for you as well. What does it mean? One schoolroom recognizes the fact that a classmate wishes to pretend he is a truck and, it seems to me, the heavens must rejoice."

"You do make it seem rather grand," she says doubtfully. "He may not be a truck anymore, you know."

"I expect he won't," I say. "Maybe *that* story was fully told and he's moved on to another. We'll see."

"What happened with the helicopter boy?" Minna asks. "How long did he remain a helicopter?"

"I don't know. The family moved to Oregon. But years later, a friend of mine visited them and told me that Jason, now a teenager, could not remember being a helicopter and, in fact, had no interest in machinery of any kind. So, for one year he had to be a helicopter and then went on to something else. I wish I'd been there to see how it happened. Once I asked a girl in our school about Jason. She had been his closest supporter during his helicopter days and was now in sixth grade. She could not recall anyone who had pretended all year to be a helicopter, yet she remembered a lot of other things from preschool days, including a long period of doll-corner play with Jason as her baby. You see, these matters are quite mysterious and beyond convenient analysis."

By the time I describe the upcoming adventure to my husband, I experience a few doubts of my own. Am I really planning to drive hundreds of miles in order to find out if a seven-year-old is still a truck? Actually, when the time comes, I fly there instead.

On the plane, I read, in a novel by Annie Dillard, the following remarkable truth: "No child on earth was ever meant to be ordinary, and you can see it in them, and they know it, too, but then the times get to them, and they wear out their brains learning what folks expect, and spend their strength trying to rise over those same folks."

"Do you always give the children titles?" Minna asks gaily. "As though they are books?" We are driving from the airport and I have asked again about the boy who would be a truck.

The notion is intriguing. "Well, why not? What if we do consider each child a book, ready to be written? School life would be rather more dramatic, wouldn't it?"

Minna looks worried. "Dear me, I'm afraid you're going to find us dull. There's not much excitement here, except maybe during hunting season." She points to bags of "deer apples" for sale along the road, entice-ments for the hunted animals. "Even my husband, the most peaceful man I know, gets caught up in the com-motion. We'll have our share of venison in the freezer and all the tall tales that go with it."

In her log house on the lake, Minna starts a fire as soon as we arrive. An unexpected October blizzard has abruptly changed autumn into winter but there is no danger of running out of firewood. As with most of the neighbors, Minna tells me, she and her husband have inherited a woodlot that keeps them well supplied no matter how long or fierce the winter. They call it "har-vesting the trees."

"We're pretty self-sufficient about such things," Minna comments. "We couldn't any of us afford to pay for all the wood we require. My husband and his brothers and cousins bring it by the truckload up to the camp, too." The "camp" turns out to be a primitive enclosure, deep in the woods, used for hunting and fishing, that is also part of every family's history. The people with whom I will spend the better part of the coming week are quite at home in the outdoors.

By comparison, my husband and I more resemble Gertrude Warner's runaway siblings in *The Boxcar Children* who fashion a temporary home out of an abandoned railroad car in the woods. We are really city folks, born and bred, which is probably why I cannot get to the heart of pine trees and herons in my writing.

Nonetheless, I have as much in common with Minna in a classroom as with any city teachers I know. We both harvest children who choose to be trucks and helicopters, princesses and superheroes, kittens and rabbits, and who welcome the even less likely preferences of others. City or country, life is a story into which one comes in disguise, the children fervently believe.

Rabbis in the Middle Ages must have marveled at their children's apparent tolerance of a wide variety of behaviors and wondered about the moral implications of this instinctive compassion. Centuries later, the Swiss psychologist Jean Piaget was to wonder about another set of truths as he observed his own children at play. And now, here are Minna and I, in timeless fashion, fascinated by the intimation of larger meanings in a boy who pretends to be a truck.

"The fire feels good," Minna says, setting down a tray of cookies and coffee. As she begins to describe her school, my uncertainties about coming disappear. There are fewer than one hundred students in the kindergarten through eighth grade and she knows them all. We have nearly ten times that number in my school and I can remember only a fraction besides those who were in my own classroom. Minna also can name and tell me something about everyone's cousins, aunts, uncles, grandparents, and, in some cases, great-grandparents.

Her own grandparents emigrated from Finland a decade after mine came from Russia, hers to this sparsely inhabited region and mine to noisy tenements in a crowded city. They all struggled to put food on the table and keep everyone warm in the winter and found the new world not much kinder than the old. But our families must have tried to make it so, for here we sit,

Minna and I, first-born Americans, coming together to explore further ways to dignify life in a classroom.

Walking on the beach the day we met, I recited the "moral universe" passage to Minna and she was visibly moved. "We have a similar saying in Finnish," she told me. "My grandfather spoke no English and was a strict Lutheran. He was also quite fond of children. He used to say something about angels speaking through the mouths of children. He'd say this when one of us was particularly unselfish or kind, maybe unexpectedly so. But when we were naughty he would warn us that the angels would not tell stories about what we had just done. I'd feel sad then. I wanted so to be worthy of an angel's stories."

I remind Minna now of what she said that day on the beach about her grandfather and the stories angels tell. "Would Timmy and his truck qualify for the angels?" I ask and we both laugh, neither of us willing to speak for the angels.

That night, lying awake listening to the waves crash against the rocks, I try to imagine what an angel might say about the boy who would be a helicopter, but my dreams are far more inclusive. Harry and Teddy enter the scene and Tovah too is there, bringing one child after the other into her joyful dance around the classroom.

When I meet the teachers the next morning I state my goal: two stories each from every kindergarten, first-, and second-grade child, acted out the day they are told. Even Minna is skeptical that such an ambitious-sounding plan can succeed, but I know how quickly the process goes. Once the children see that their stories can be told and dramatized in so simple a manner, the incentive is great and a good rhythm is easily established.

Furthermore, I point out, the regular classroom activities need not be interrupted while the children come to me one at a time. Then, at a convenient break in the schedule, we will gather around a rug to act out the stories told thus far. This is what I wait for, seeing the pleasure on the storytellers' faces when *their* words are taken up by others, followed immediately by the actor's gratitude in being able to carry out another child's fantasy. It is this effect I have traveled such a distance to witness again.

I know which child is Timmy as soon as I enter the second-grade classroom. His anxiously lowered eyes and frantic search for the Lego container reminds me of what the helicopter boy might have done when a strange adult suddenly appeared. The others are curious about me and the activity I bring them but Timmy steers clear of the story table as if it were a trap.

My disappointment is rapidly replaced by pure enjoyment as the storytelling proceeds. This is the first time since leaving my own school that I will be able to record the spontaneous outpouring of an entire classroom of children and, except for Timmy, every child has signed up. It will take two visits to complete the first set of stories and the remaining two days to do the second set. The sweetness of anticipation builds with each new story and the comforting knowledge that, yes, it is all going the way it is supposed to go. And yet, there are still two questions I cannot now, nor have I ever been able to answer: Why are the children so certain they must tell me a story and why is there such excitement over the opportunity to have their classmates become the characters in their stories? Is it, perhaps, positive proof, in word and deed, of one's acceptance? The infant returns a smile; the schoolchild returns a story. If I am smiled at and dramatized then I am loved, I am safe, I am not invisible.

One thing is clear: no matter how inelegantly a story is told, or how shaky the sequence of events, the children value each other's offerings and want to be part of the event. There is a glow to these child audiences as they wait to touch and sound out the inner thoughts of another child. In my journal this night I will claim an aura of communal salvation in the day's proceedings, but I tend to grow expansive in my late night writing.

And yet, this storytelling and story acting symbolizes something larger and more primary in the universe than merely the sum of its tales. In the telling and recreating of the stories there is a sense of the open-handedness of other children; the loneliness and isolation inherent in the schoolhouse is often relieved only by their curiosity and spontaneity. They are not always kind, as we know. They are, however, on the edge of kindness, ready and waiting for an opening.

"Hey, man," Damone tells Albert. "Come on, you can do it, Albert my man, watch me, sh-sh-sh, do what I'm showing you." The moral universe rested then on Damone, though a week later his mother came to help govern his behavior. But during Damone's shining hour he gave Albert the words he needed and a lifeline back into the group. This must have been the moment when the angels captured his story and proclaimed Damone as one of their very own.

The teachers are eager to see how I do this thing I have come to do, and so I use the first story dictated in each classroom as a demonstration for the children and teachers alike. Once the children view the sequence of telling and acting, they seldom need further encouragement. In Timmy's class, Allen volunteers so quickly I wonder if he has done this before, but he tells me he has not.

"There were three deer," he begins, staring at the snow covering a distant field. "They were eating the corn." His attention is drawn to my hand rushing across the page and he slows down to match my pace. "And then they heard footsteps; it was a bear. So they ran away, but there was another bear. They were trapped." Allen measures my reaction and is satisfied that he has me in suspense. "So they split up and found a way out and they ran home."

When the class assembles around the rug, Allen seems shy. "I guess I'll be the bear," he mumbles, growling appropriately, thought not as loudly as he will later when he agrees to be the bear in another child's story. The four actors required to complete Allen's cast come forward without hesitation. No doubt they have dramatized storybooks before, but not a classmate's spontaneous story. There is no preparation or lines to learn; one simply follows a narration that sounds like any child's ordinary speech. No wonder those in the audience are willing to accept almost any sort of role, one by one, around the rug. It is as natural as play itself and all are given a fair chance to be in the spotlight.

Timmy, absorbed in his Lego construction on the other side of the room, refuses the bait. I keep glancing his way, wondering if he is listening, projecting my voice toward him. Fortunately, the teacher is not aware of my concern or she might feel obliged to bring him to the rug. Then I would not know the effect of the storytelling on Timmy. In any case, the fate of my un-defined search cannot rest upon the response of one child, even someone who understands the meaning of becoming a truck.

The other children discover everything they need to know as they watch and take part in Allen's story. Had I asked anything else of them on such short notice, many would have resisted. As it is, fifteen of the sixteen chil-dren have signed up to tell a story. The single holdout acts as if he is unaware of the activity.

Quickly we begin. I am the scribe, they are the play-wrights. Pages fill with unicorns and butterflies, mon-sters and hungry cougars, lost kittens and princesses, ravens and eagles, plus the ghosts and pumpkins of the Halloween season. Relieved of the need to do their own writing, ideas flow as in a dream. A roomful of imagi-nations has been released. Even the prosaic "Me and my mom went to the store" requires a commitment to fantasy: *pretend* this is me, pretend this is my mom, pretend this is the store. The *pretend* raises every action to heightened analysis on a plane where nothing is what it appears to be.

Whatever the plot, there is an overlay of the untamed outdoors, far more than I am used to, and less television imagery. Almost none, in fact. But the basic themes of children's play are there: someone is alone and a friend comes; someone is in trouble and help is on the way. "There was three puppies. They ran away from home and almost got eaten by a cougar. Then they got caught up in a tornado. And they lived."

They live and, more often then not, are kept safe. "Me and my dog are going trick or treating. We went to a spooky house that had a ghost. We ran home and my mom saved us." Aaron, who tells the story, does not live with his mother but knows how he would like things to be. In his second story, the next day, the dog does not find his way home. When that story is acted out, a girl reaches over and touches Aaron's arm sympathetically. The sight of her response lifts me to another realm. If Teddy were here he would know the full meaning of what has taken place in a fraction of a second.

Timmy might be similarly affected were he with us on the rug. Like the San tribal member who is away,

Timmy has missed a piece of the group story; that part of him is lost. What is his home story, I wonder. People here do not reveal such matters to strangers, which is a good thing. I notice he has not spoken to anyone but the teacher since I entered the room, yet these are the classmates who once climbed on the back of his truck. That persona gave Timmy a dependable pattern of breaking and fixing. Can a Lego set supply the same courage and optimism? Has Timmy found a *visible* role to play and does it have the potential to include others? Harry could seldom tolerate intrusions into his block play but in his stories he reached out to all of us. We raised our arms, pretending to be the sun, while Harry frolicked with other puppies on the rug that was our stage.

Having promised myself I would exert no pressure on Timmy, nonetheless, during a break in the stories I approach him, notebook in hand. My voice sounds insincere as I bend low to speak. I deserve the response I receive. "Timmy, excuse me, I know you didn't sign up, but if you did tell a story, what would it be about?"

It is too late to swallow my words. Timmy frowns, not looking up. "About three ducks," he intones so quietly I can barely hear. "One is killed and the others die."

He turns away, his fingers moving rapidly over the

tiny plastic shapes. I have been rejected and it is painful. I thank him for the story but do not write it down. The fact is, I can't figure out what to do with a story I have coerced from a child. Shall I pretend I have not heard it?

Angie waits patiently at the story table. My face is hot and my hands are sweaty. "Once there was a unicorn and butterflies," she begins, cooling me with peaceful images. "They played all day in the meadow." My breathing has returned to normal and I smile at the mass of dark curls hiding the storyteller's face. "Then one day a monster ate up the unicorn. But she kicked at him and he ran away. The end."

"Was she still inside the monster?" Johanna asks, looking up from her drawing. "You have to make her jump out."

Angie glances at her friend and considers the option. "Yeah, the unicorn jumps out," she directs me to add, "and she runs home. But no one is there." Thus she satisfies her friend but leaves the outcome in doubt.

Proust would not have allowed a friend to influence him as Angie does. In *The Guermantes Way* he writes, "Ideas are goddesses who deign at times to make themselves visible to a solitary mortal at a turning point in the road . . . but as soon as a companion joins him they vanish. In the society of his fellows no man has ever beheld them."

This may be so for the mature artist but not for Angie and Johanna, nor for the other youthful story-tellers I have known over the years. Their stories depend on the interference, which is to say, on the kindness of children. When joined by a companion, loneliness vanishes, allowing goddesses to step forward and play a part in their story.

Angie's ready acceptance of another child's interest and counsel revives my hopes for Timmy. Watching him hunched up in the corner, I know he will not long remain a solitary Lego builder. A child resilient enough to pull out of danger and recreate himself as a truck will find another role among the puppies who defy cougars and the unicorns who jump out of the jaws of monsters. Furthermore, no one seems to be hurrying Timmy to *become* something; there will be time in this school to establish a new story about himself.

I walk down the hallway to the kindergarten. The five-year-olds accept my offer to record their stories as enthusiastically as the second graders, perhaps more so. Several of them step onto the rug with each story, certain they are called upon to act each role. When one puppy is needed five may appear.

There seems little doubt, however, as to their reason for telling a story; the plots they invent have entirely to do with play, whether with siblings, pets, or friends. Most of these kindergartners have not been to school before. They are in school now for a mere two-and-a-half hours but they understand that in a story they can pretend to play with someone. A character who has no one to play with is in trouble; the children take this as a given.

Karl plops beside me, knowing instantly what he wants to say. "I like my brother to play with me outside." He stands up, the task completed; the one-sentence story will serve as our demonstration. Evan, chosen to be the brother, and Karl stare at each other across the rug; then, at a mutually definable moment they clasp hands and run about in circles.

The thirteen children sitting around the rug perceive every unspoken line. Let me be your brother too, their eyes plead. But it is Teddy's face I see.

Much to my surprise, I meet Karl's brother an hour later in Minna's first-grade classroom. His name is Frank. We are about to act out his story of a dragon who exhales fire and two friends ready to poke at him with swords, when I say, "Your brother Karl put you in his story."

"My little brother? How'd he do that?" Everyone else is equally surprised so I show them Karl's story, recorded just as theirs has been, in my handwriting. "I like my brother to play with me outside," I read. "Would you like to act it out as Karl did?"

"Naw," comes his embarrassed reply. "Just do mine."

"Maybe it's your other brothers he means," someone suggests. "No way!" Frank explodes. "I'm the onliest one plays with him. He comes to me 'cause he knows I'll say yes 'cause I always do."

The room is silent. We have just received information of enormous importance, creating a similar bond between the children as when Luis said his brothers were mean to him. The telling of either side of this elemental tale of sibling relationships brings a group together in mysterious ways. Frank himself is affected. "Yeah, okay, we can do Karl's story." The scene lasts but a moment yet something has been released into the atmosphere that changes the group as we begin Frank's story.

"Me and my friend Sam saw a dragon in the forest and I fight it with my sword and . . ." Frank interrupts my reading. "Can I put my brother in this?" he asks. "Me and Sam and *Karl* is there and we got a shield to protect us when the dragon blows fire." An additional actor, representing Karl, enters the stage and the play continues.

In bed at night I think about Teddy, wondering if he has a brother or sister to play with him and protect him from the dragon's fiery breath. One day of storytelling has gone by and my mind runs over with brothers and sisters, past and present. "Be my brother," Damone urges Albert. Harry often began a story with "The puppy digged under the fence to find his brothers." The number of little girls lost in the woods who find an unknown sister would fill volumes. The need to re-enact family, real or imagined, is instinctive and powerful. Proust repeats the scene of his mother coming up the stairs to kiss him goodnight, and Karl returns to the theme of brother as playmate in his next two stories. This is the central fact we are to know about him: he is the boy who plays with his brother Frank.

"Frank put me in his story," Karl informs me the next day. "And a dragon. He told our mommy." News travels fast in a family. I can almost see their mother's pleasure, knowing that her sons are somehow connected in a new school activity. Now Karl continues on his own track as if no other stories have intervened. "Then me and Frank play with the dogs," he says, handing me paper and pencil.

Storytellers, it would seem, are in the business of passing on favors. Two brothers tell stories about each other and their mother beams with pride. The favors are bestowed upon both sets of classmates as well, for they gain a view of brotherly affection and sense the possibility for family to enter the domain of school life.

Another favor is due: I want Timmy to hear the stories told by two brothers in school. Do I overstep some unseen boundary? How can this be the case when it is the children's own words I bring to each new audience? If there is any unnatural separation it is the one between home and school, not between the children.

"I have a story to pass on to you," I tell the second graders. "Three, actually. Two are from Karl in the kindergarten and one from his brother Frank, in first grade."

The children smile at Simon. "That's my cousins," he tells me. Timmy looks up from his Lego set. Do I imagine a slight upward curve to his mouth?

The students listen intently as the brothers' stories appear to form a single narrative, and Timmy sets his gaze directly upon me, for the first time. He stands up, grabs a handful of Legos, and comes to the story table.

Today's visit takes place during free time and my table fills with all manner of artists and spectators. As each storyteller proceeds, there is a murmuring accompaniment: a phrase repeated, suggestions offered, approval displayed. Unlike Proust's solitary thinker, the children's ideas take wing in the company of their peers. When one is young, the need to be discovered is greater than the desire for privacy. I feel included in the process; after a day and a half of storytelling, I am no longer a stranger.

"There was a unicorn," Holly dictates, and instantly a horn appears on a crayoned figure across the table. "It didn't have a friend," Holly continues, penciling her own unicorn in the margin of the story paper, colliding gently with my hand as I write her words. We smile at each other. "Then she found a deer to play with."

Holly exchanges seats with Doyle whose story is next. "My deer might get eaten," he tells Holly, who shrugs and searches for a crayon in the bin. "There was a deer," Doyle dictates, "and there was a cougar in a tree. The deer walked underneath where the cougar was and he pounced down fast. He ate the deer."

Holly adds a flower to her picture; she must have

known that Doyle's deer would suffer a different fate from hers. Does it bother Holly as Timmy's duck story affected me? I am certain she prefers the next story told by Eddie. "Along came a deer and it was drinking in the pond. Then he lays down in the meadow. And then the other deers come because the cougar is gone." The storytellers have entered a communal dance, moving toward each other, then away, then back together.

Nicole has been observing the subtle dramas. "Mine's like Holly's," she promises. "There was a little rabbit that was lonely. And somebody played with her. And they were happy. Especially the little rabbit because she was lonely and then . . ."

"Somebody who?" Timmy interrupts, squeezing in next to Nicole. "A deer," she explains. "Mine's like Holly I said."

Timmy glances at the drawings on either side of him and begins his own. He works fast, as Harry did, and soon a ship appears, half submerged in a rough sea. Harry's boat would not be sinking but the two boys are uncommonly alike as artists, moving over a page with wave-like motions, filling in bits of color only after the sketch is done.

Anthony has begun a story, his second. Yesterday he made himself captain of an ore boat that struck an iceberg. Valiantly, he went down with the ship and "the ore poured into the water." It was then I realized I had written "oar boat," not knowing that in this part of the world boats carry iron ore. "I made a mistake, Anthony," I said, erasing the word. "I guess I've never been told a story about an ore boat before." He smiled at me graciously but he must have been curious about an adult who lacks such knowledge.

In any case, today's story contains more explanatory material and offers a happier finale. "The ore boat picks up some ore in Alaska and when they were heading back the captain noticed something white. It was an iceberg. But he turned the boat before it could break. And then he made a remarkable recovery of a sunken treasure ship."

Anthony takes his time, drawing pictures as he goes along. First there is the ore boat, then the jagged iceberg, and finally the captain pointing ahead, his mouth forming an O-shaped scream. Though we are past the scheduled cut-off time, I do not rush Anthony along. Timmy watches us both from across the table.

"Where's *my* story?" he asks when Anthony stands up. "I told one yesterday."

"I didn't write it down, Timmy. I thought you didn't want me to."

"I did." Timmy repeats the story, following each word I print. "It's about the ducks. One is killed and the others die." No one at the table seems surprised by the story and, moments later, when we act it out, Timmy and two other solemn-faced ducks squawk, flutter, and die.

"Good story," Anthony says, and there is a general nodding around the rug. Apparently a valid scene has been portrayed. Stories in which bad things happen are given their due in this group.

Walking along the beach after school, bundled up against the frigid winds, I wonder about the value I place on "good" stories. Timmy's duck story is as much appreciated as Karl's tale of brotherly love, maybe because it acknowledges deeply contrasting emotions. At any given moment, when an entire group tells stories, someone is blending fact with fantasy, joy with sadness, the most ordinary rituals with unexpected outcomes. The cumulative effect must be profound, each child making personal sense of all the unspoken messages.

These spontaneous storytellers create little homes for one another where everyone can imagine playing a role and no one is left out. Every story is a piece of the whole and none is complete without the others. Perhaps the reason children are eager to take part in one another's stories is so they may fill in the empty spaces. Good deeds make sense only after someone's suffering is perceived, and three dead ducks pave the way for unicorns who find playmates and deer who snooze safely in peaceful meadows.

During the remaining two days, I continue shuttling between classrooms, adding the special education class to my schedule. Boundaries created by age, skill, and experience disappear as the stories provide our content and continuity. I have fleeting images of the Hasidic storyteller, going from village to village, reporting the deeds of holy people in story form. Yet my work consists only of transmitting the scenes that occur to a single child onto a makeshift stage for all to view. Before I leave, every child will have told at least two stories, witnessed and acted out by the entire group.

These are not ordinary events; there is a feeling in the school that something unusual is taking place. Teachers in other grades have begun to stop by and several make a point of telling me what they see. In so doing, more often than not, they reveal a piece of their own stories. A high-school girl who helps out in the first grade during her free period tells me privately, "If I had done this when I was little, I wouldn't be so shy in school. I always worry about speaking out in class." Later I meet her in the hall and she beams at me. "Guess what? I asked if I could take down stories when I come and Minna said yes. She's my cousin, you know."

I didn't know, but somehow the information does not surprise me. Since the day I met Minna on the beach and we talked about the boy who would be a truck, I felt the presence of connections reaching out in all directions and pulling us together.

Certain children have already established titles in my mind but I don't remark upon this to Minna. We do not interpret students to each other, allowing them to represent themselves in their stories and conversations. Since all stories are dictated to me, I am generally un-aware of the reading or writing skills of my storytellers. I know only such personal information as they deign to impart.

Charles quickly becomes "the boy who would be a policeman." His first story is about himself and a po-liceman named Mr. Anderson: "Mr. Anderson lets me use all his uniforms and he shows me where the bad guys are. Every day he takes me to arrest a bad guy." A day later Charles tells a story in which he himself will be Mr. Anderson, father of three: "My little kids wanted some of my stuff so I got them plastic police stuff. They wanted everything a policeman has and I let them have it."

Today Charles runs to the story table the moment I appear. I see that his name is first on the list. He smooths his hair, sits up straight, and speaks out in a loud voice, holding his hands as if on a steering wheel. "I was the patrol policeman and I saw somebody who was driving too fast. I put my patrol lights on and took him to the police station." Charles wonders if his story should be longer and I tell him it is just right for acting out, which is true. The children enjoy dramatizing a single scene. They seldom present a complex set of events, preferring to view one or two ideas at a time and alter the perspective in succeeding stories.

Holly is "the girl who would be a unicorn." In her original story the unicorn is lonely until a deer comes along. One story later, the roles are reversed and it is the deer who has no friend. In today's story the unicorn dies and "everyone is sad until a new unicorn came." Holly will be the old and the new unicorn; it is *her* role, no matter how she defines it.

I read Charles's and Holly's stories to Timmy's class just to make a point: some children like to be the same character over and over. The second graders nod, knowing this to be true. Seating myself at the story table, I note that Timmy's name is still not on the list. He is, however, at the table, with six Lego pieces, paper, and crayons, doing something I find rather unusual. He builds a structure and copies it, then dismantles the Legos and begins again, drawing facsimiles of each figure.

Anthony, "the boy who would be an ore boat captain," correctly identifies Timmy's drawing of ducks. "You gonna shoot them down?" he asks, but there is no response from Timmy who has begun to move his page of flying ducks back and forth on the table.

Meanwhile the stories accumulate and with them my secret titles for their authors. Frank is the boy who slays dragons and Helen is the girl who saves kittens from pouncing mountain lions and Jilly must always be a spotted deer. Her stories end on a worrisome note: "Then a hunter came." There is no further explanation and none is asked for; the children understand the precarious nature of life in the wild.

What else do they understand that eludes me? If only I could remain among these children and discover more of what the stories reveal, but it is enough that *they* will find out the meaning behind the stories, side by side, day after day. "Why do some children always take the same role in their stories?" I asked Frank after his third dragon story. "It's on their mind," he said. "Is it a good thing?" I went further. "Yeah, 'cause then you know who someone is."

Timmy does not tell me a story on this day. But he brings his picture to the rug, perhaps imagining his Lego ducks on the stage. Are they to be shot down or do they fly away unharmed? Is Timmy the hunter or the hunted? Why can't he simply tell me his story and resolve my anxiety? This last question is accompanied by my involuntary smile; at least I am willing to admit to being "the teacher who must find out who Timmy is" whether it makes sense or not.

But then Timmy surprises me by handing me his picture as I am about to leave the room. "He likes me," I say to myself and the thought quickens my stride. "Yes, even though he didn't tell me a story, he likes me." Is *this* what it is all about? If you tell me your story, you like me?

I hold up Timmy's picture in the first grade. "I forgot to ask Timmy if this is a story," I say. Alton, "the boy who pounces" is certain it is. "A cougar is going to pounce on them and they fly away," he says confidently.

Charles shakes his head. "No, see, there's a hunter." I

hadn't noticed the tiny figure in the right-hand corner. "But that guy has to get a ticket because it's out of season for ducks."

"No, the cougar is there, in the tree. You can't see him." Alton's stories are all about cougars and mountain lions who pounce on each other. Alton himself often assumes a crouching position as he goes about his occupations in school. Twice I have heard someone warn, "Alton, there's a lion in that tree, watching you," whereupon Alton narrows his eyes and stalks his enemy.

The next morning, my last, Timmy repeats the duck picture, then superimposes clouds over the figures. "These guys fly into the clouds," he tells Anthony who sits beside him drawing another ore boat on its way to a distant iceberg.

"I showed your pictures to the first graders, Timmy," I say. "Alton thinks a cougar pounced on the ducks and they flew away. But Charles said a hunter was trying to shoot them out of season and a policeman would give him a ticket."

Timmy stares at me, wide-eyed. Then he laughs, a huge laugh, that seems to explode all around him. And he keeps laughing. A vision of Tovah, dancing in joy, appears before me. There are fragile connections here, to be glimpsed and wondered at, but not defined. At least not by me.

"Was Timmy ever a truck while you were there?" Minna asks as we drive to the airport. We avoided the topic the entire time I was in her home.

"No, never a truck. He was a Lego builder and he draws pictures of sinking boats and ducks, like the one I brought to your classroom. It's quite complicated. I have no name for Timmy, none at all."

"Then I guess he seems more ordinary now."

"Not that either," I reply. "Maybe the others seem less ordinary. It was quite sobering, in a way. Since I knew the children only through their stories, they began to appear as different from one another as Timmy did."

I would like to say more about Timmy but nothing I could tell Minna would be even half the truth. If I knew exactly why Timmy laughed, I might be able to pull all my thoughts together. If I knew why Tovah danced or why Edmond had to have Teddy in his story then perhaps I would understand how it all pertains to the moral universe. If I knew why Harry ran down the hall to bring cookies to Martin and why Damone stopped everything in order to give Albert the words he needed, if I knew all these things, could I even then name the unnamed?

On the other hand, were I to discover the answers to these questions, the story would be over. It is not time for me to close the classroom door.

Several weeks later, I am in a Manhattan school for girls, once again asking children to act out their stories for one another. I will be there for only a day and this makes me sad. I fear I can never again be satisfied with less than all the children's stories; and yet, I tell myself, it took such a brief time for Teddy and Tovah to become part of my life.

I have brought several stories from Minna's school to use as a demonstration. "The children who dictated these stories live on farms, surrounded by dense forests," I say. "I'll write to them and send some of your stories in return."

As Holly's unicorn and Alton's crouching cougar prepare the stage for new dramas, the idea of making up a little story in order to act it out is grasped enthusiastically. The girl who would be Luke Skywalker and the girl who would be a princess are the first storytellers, followed by lost kittens and puppies having birthdays with unexpected friends. Robbers are sighted from afar, and mean people disappear into elevators. There are no hunters, ore boats, or deer in these New York stories, but a number of lost and found characters along with mommies, ballet dancers, and doormen.

A kindergarten girl dictates, "My baby sister lets me play with her," and a second grader says, "Once there was a girl lost in the woods and she found a baby brother who didn't have a mother or father." As the stories accumulate, a sense of timelessness overtakes the brevity of an individual encounter: I have been here before, each succeeding story reveals, yet every word seems new to my ears.

There is no time, of course, to exchange as many stories between classes as I did in Minna's school, but after the first period, I have an indigenous set of stories to use in the next grade. "I know her!" cries a second grader upon hearing a kindergartner's story. "She's my sister's friend." As always, when such a connection is made, there is a heightened interest from others. How we yearn for these ties to be clearly displayed once we leave home. We cannot long tolerate a feeling of disconnectedness; if we are unable to bring in our own sibling, someone else's will do.

After a particularly intimate story from Ruthie in which she and her sisters are allowed to watch TV in their parents' king-size bed, Sarah reacts sharply, much as Luis did when confronted with too many "good" stories. "I had the worst nightmare, the horriblest ever," she tells us, then cautions me *not* to write it down. "Two bad guys in long beards stoled my mother in the night and put her in a bag and threw her down the incinerator. I tried to find 911 on the phone but I couldn't see the numbers."

We stare at Sarah while Margaret waits, not knowing whether to begin her story. Sarah's nightmare seems to have taken up all the space at the table. I recall Harry's terrifying dream told years earlier. Hadn't his mother been dragged away in a car by bearded men?

I nod to Margaret. "I am in my bed," she states quietly. Immediately she has everyone's attention. "I am dreaming. I am dreaming about a garden. The garden has birds and flowers. Everything there is calm and quiet. I like to be there. When I'm lonely my friends come with me at night."

Margaret is not finished, but she looks directly at Sarah as she continues her dream. "The place I am dreaming of has everything you would need but not nightmares. Nightmares are not good in this special place. Because this special place has friends and no violence."

The children begin to laugh and, after a moment, I am laughing too, remembering the girl in Harry's class who had given us just such a dream to counteract his nightmare. Here it is again, the incredible ability of children to create moments of hopefulness for one another, to explain in secret or open ways that somewhere there is a garden with birds and flowers, where everything is calm and quiet, and there are no nightmares. And that when we are lonely, a friend will come.

However, something else has suddenly been revealed to me. It is not so much the content of a story that is so uplifting to the children but rather the realization that they are able to make up stories and imagine themselves inside the stories of other children. This act of creation, repeated over and over, opens each day to the wondrous possibilities of good things happening, just when it may seem that all is lost. If Harry knows that the sun is shining and the puppies are playing, we need not despair. We are safe for another day.

Rosy-cheeked Caroline sits beside me in a London kindergarten, her eyes following the progression of words along the page as she speaks. "One day a little girl and a little boy went to a big forest but they didn't know if it had bad things or good things. It was a brother and a sister." She moves her finger along the s-i-s-t-e-r. "So there was nothing that was bad. But they didn't know if there was."

Her wide-eyed look of wonder reminds me of Teddy, though perhaps this is because I am once again in London, and he is much on my mind. Nearly two years have passed since I watched Teddy's tremulous approach toward an unknown group of children. He must have wondered, as Caroline does, if good or bad things would happen. For him the answer lay in the imaginative power of young children doling out their invented roles without regard to such superficial differences as wheelchairs and padded helmets.

Now Caroline must decide the fate of characters she herself has brought into being. Will she carry them to safety or allow them to suffer? My pencil awaits midair but Caroline is silent. After a few moments I ask, "Shall I read your story back to you? To see if you want to say more?"

I review the text, pronouncing the final sentence slowly. "So there was nothing that was bad but they didn't know if there was." Caroline shakes her head; the story is done. She does not leave the table, however, wanting to hear the other storytellers. What will she learn from their private visions and public disguises?

"The cat smelled the flowers and the dog smelled the

leaves but they didn't smell their owner. Then he came."

"A bat went up to the moon by himself. No one would help him. Then he found a spaceship."

"The egg cracked open and the baby dinosaur looked and looked but he could not find his mum. Then his dad came."

"There was a tiger but nobody liked him. Then he saw a frog that was looking at him nicely."

Caroline and her classmates come from a very different world than the children in Minna's school. Their families are likely to move to a new country every few years, propelled by the international interests of corporations and governments, whereas Minna and her neighbors have lived in the same place for three generations. Yet both sets of children explore similar issues of displacement and loneliness as each child tries to discover if the forest is good or bad.

It is Jordan's turn to tell a story. "The little frog had no one to play with. They didn't like him. His leg wasn't long enough and he didn't jump proper."

Involuntarily I glance at Jordan's legs, unable to tell if he can "jump proper". Young storytellers, of course, are well versed in the use of metaphor but something tells me Jordan knows something of the frog's dilemma.

Caroline is interested in Jordan's story, placing her finger on the word frog. "F-r-o-g," she spells. Then, turning to me, she declares, "I didn't finish my story," waiting while I retrieve her paper from the pile in front of me.

"I fed my cat tuna fish," she begins. "His name is Gus. I was three when I did it, in my old house. Then when I got down off my stool, Gus got up by my leg and rub rub rubbed my leg. 'Cause we were so happy that time."

"Is this still about the brother and sister in the forest?" I ask.

She is surprised by my question. "Gus is in the forest," is her quiet reply.

We smile at Caroline, imagining the feel of a warm kitten. Even the youngest of these schoolchildren understand why Gus has to be in Caroline's forest. Other things will be there too, some in the shadows and some in the sunlight. That is why we keep telling our stories, so that inevitably we will arrive at the good part of the forest.

Before leaving London I call Janice Eliot in whose classroom I had once been mesmerized by a boy in a wheelchair and by the kindness of children. Janice tells me she is on sabbatical and the baby gurgling into the phone is three-month-old Adam.

"As you see, a great deal has happened to me since your visit. But I remember Teddy well, though he came only another six weeks or so. The family moved, because of the father's work."

She excuses herself to put the baby into his cradle and when she returns says, "You were quite taken with Teddy, weren't you?"

"Not only Teddy but with your children as well. I was there the first time he saw their stories acted out, when they insisted he take the role of a little puppy who hadn't yet learned to walk."

Janice seems grateful for the opportunity to talk about Teddy. "You know, it was quite remarkable. His teachers thought so too. Those stories were on Teddy's mind whenever he came. And furthermore, his participation heightened the importance of the activity. 'Is Teddy coming today?' the children would ask. If so, several would include a red car in their stories. As soon as Teddy's group arrived, they'd remind the driver to bring his car. As far as they were concerned he could take *any* role as long as he had the car. And here's something that will surprise you, Vivian. Before he left he brought us a story of his own."

The information does startle me. "But how—?"

"Apparently, he dictated the story to an older sister. Wouldn't you love to have seen how he did it, struggling as he did with one word at a time?"

"It's hard to imagine. His sister must understand his every motion and sound." A vision intrudes of Teddy flailing his arms, his entire body, straining to speak. "Do you remember the story?"

"Every word. It was only one sentence. 'Robin and Batman are in the batmobile chasing a bad guy.' He was Robin."

"Teddy is Robin?" Instantly the vision before me is transformed. There is Teddy in mask and cape, flying through the air with Batman at his side.

"And, by the way," Janice adds, "the children weren't at all surprised, almost as if they'd known all along of his true identity."

The children and Teddy have fulfilled the injunction: It is not in heaven. Teddy's disguise is accepted even as is his despair. And Teddy, returning the favor, puts his dream into a story.

"That don't change a thing, man," insisted Stanley in Reverend Flambeau's high-school English class. "You get right back to being angry soon enough." But then Tovah told us her story and danced, and we were all so happy for a while.

Several months have passed. The peregrinations of Teddy's story fill a number of notebooks, which I bring along on a visit to an old friend, expecting to read a few sections to her. However, her granddaughter has something on her mind that takes precedence and puts Teddy on hold.

Eight-year-old Carrie and I sit on a porch swing at dusk, a good place and time for secrets. She gives the swing a vigorous push, then asks a riddle that has the sound of a personal disclosure. "What do you look for every day and sometimes you think you found it, but then the next day you have to start looking again? I'll give you a hint. It's about school."

Her riddle will not be a funny one. She has been telling me she doesn't like third grade. "Let's see. Is it when you answer a math problem and then the next day you have to do it again?"

Carrie looks at me doubtfully. "Okay, here's another hint. It's sort of like that book Grandma showed me. The one you wrote about you can't tell people not to play with you?"

"The children do that to you, Carrie?"

"I'll tell you the riddle," she says. "Every day you look for someone who likes you and sometimes you think you found a friend, but the next day you have to start again."

I put an arm around Carrie and wait. She has more to say but once the words are spoken they can no longer be disguised as a riddle. The soothing motion of the swing and enveloping darkness on the porch give her courage.

"The kids hate me," she says simply. Four decades of teaching do not lessen the shock of her words. "They told me why. We even had a meeting about it. The teacher said they're being mean but anyway they kept on arguing with her."

Carrie speaks rapidly. Her story must be gotten out before the door closes. "Here's why they hate me so much. The way I talk. And my laugh is stupid. And I never get a joke so I have this dumb look on my face they can't stand. Stuff like that they were saying. And because I cry."

"Your teacher should not have allowed this, Carrie."

"She *told* them they were wrong. And they were giving their *opinions*."

"No, Carrie, honey, believe me, those are not opinions. When one person copies another without thinking, it is not an opinion. None of the things they said are true, you know. None of this is your fault."

"That's what Mommy said."

"I'll bet some of the children felt bad about what was being said, but they didn't know how to stop it. Your teacher also didn't know how."

My Teddy stories do not balance the pain Carrie feels. This is not a time for good stories, here on this pleasant suburban porch. Carrie's experiences deserve full play, with no attempt to gloss over them.

"My mom and dad are going to talk to the teacher." She looks worried. These are difficult times for a family. Why, they wonder, should we have to defend our child from the abuse of her classmates? Isn't this the teacher's job? Yet they must tread lightly, lest the teacher think she is blamed, even though they *do* blame her.

"I'm glad your parents are going to school, Carrie. Everyone needs to become involved. This is a very serious matter."

Carrie studies my face, as if I have just told *her* a riddle. "What *is* the serious matter?" she asks.

"Here's what I think is so serious; that ordinary schoolchildren come as far as third grade thinking they have the right to gang up and hurt a classmate as they have hurt you. And the grownups don't know what to do about it. *That* part is the most serious of all."

A week later, I am surrounded by fifth graders in the

library of an elementary school in New York City. By extraordinary coincidence, it suddenly seems, they have come to talk to me about the book Carrie referred to, *You Can't Say You Can't Play.* I am grimly aware that this study of rejection written ten years earlier did not help me answer Carrie's riddle.

Mr. Moraine, the principal, has asked the students to read the book and be prepared to discuss it with me when I come there for a teacher in-service program. He stands in front of the room, waving the slim paperback. "Mrs. Paley has written this for adults," he says, "but I figure you're the adults in our school and we haven't really talked that much, as a group, about such things. Some of you told me you like the title, but just what about it do you like? I keep hearing you tell people, in one way or another, that they *cannot* play. Now who exactly is doing what to whom? And why?"

He sips from his water bottle and lowers his voice. "The fact is, a number of students at each grade are not allowed by others to be *players.* It's an accepted part of school life. Your teachers and I can't do much about it. Maybe we don't try hard enough. That's something I've been thinking about lately. Well, let's begin. Who wants to talk first?"

Jenny is ready. She is not intimidated by the principal's remarks, nor by my presence. "It's a very nice book," she says politely, "but I think your rule is sort of vague. I mean, like, what if you're not actually playing but you're doing another thing, like talking privately? Can anyone, just *any* person, I mean, *uninvited*, join you? Isn't that *rude* to do that?"

"Sure, it's probably them you're talking about, right?" Richard grins as he says this. "Look, play includes talking too, doesn't it? The *rude* one has to be the one who blows you away. That's what your rule is about, isn't it?"

He looks at me for clarification and Mr. Moraine laughs. "Richard isn't known for his vagueness, is he, class? 'Blow someone away.' *Very* visual."

"Doesn't that mean to kill someone?" I ask.

"Yeah, well, I hate to say it," Richard continues, "because I'm as guilty as anyone. But if you reject a guy isn't it a bit like you're killing him?"

Carrie knows the feeling and, from the looks on the faces of these fifth graders, so do they. Richard has named it well. Yet, something else is revealed in their faces. They will not give up the habit of blowing someone away because of a sign warning them, "You can't say you can't play." And what of the rejected ones? Will they storm the school door and demand their rights?

Nor will anyone have a change of heart, I fear, simply by hearing my Teddy stories. What sorts of illusions have overtaken me these past many months?

Jenny has another question. "You say in the book the rule works in kindergarten but those kids in fourth and fifth grade didn't think it would work for them. Did they change their minds?"

The children are surprised to hear me admit that I don't know. Amy frowns and asks, "How come?" as if I am hiding something. Why wouldn't I know? Didn't I write the book? I feel a flush spreading upwards to my face.

"I probably ought to know. But I haven't seen for myself how the rule works in older grades. The teachers and parents who write to me mostly describe children who are being rejected. And the others, who say the rule is in place in their classrooms, don't give me enough details. I'd like to know when it *doesn't* work."

I have warmed up to the subject. "You see, I realize things are not as they should be. A third grader named Carrie, in a school like yours where the rule is discussed, has just told me that her classmates *hate* her. They listed all the reasons for hating her at a class meeting."

The children are startled. Perhaps this story is too familiar. Are we really allowed to say such things? "She actually had to listen to all these silly reasons. The way she laughs, the way she talks, the way she looks when they tell her a joke."

Amy holds back tears. "They do that to my sister."

"I'm sorry to hear that, Amy," I say. "We know this makes you very sad."

Mr. Moraine moves closer to Amy. "I hadn't heard about your sister's problem. I promise I'll find out more about it."

The librarian has been listening to the discussion and now she speaks. "I have to say, Mrs. Paley, that the rule would have heavy going in our classes. This class too. These young people have pretty much been allowed to say what they will to each other. Unless you physically assault someone, there are no real consequences. Even here in the library, you'd be surprised at what I hear. I often have to keep myself from saying 'Shame on you!'"

The children shift around, changing positions on the floor while the librarian moves her gaze from child to child. "The thing is, on the playground, you kids will scream at someone if you think cheating is going on in a game. But I've never seen you stop anyone from insulting or ridiculing another person."

She turns back to me. "Please don't get me wrong.

These are great kids and I love them all. I especially love the way they get excited by books. But they are capable of hurting someone the way your friend Carrie was hurt. And that's the plain truth."

The librarian's words are not taken lightly. Some of the children have moved to chairs as if they need to be further away from each other. Then Sandy says, "It's like my dad with smoking. He knows it's a real bad habit. He says he's smoked half his life and he can't give it up. Well, we've been rejecting kids half our life just about. You can give it up easy in kindergarten because you only just started."

"People could so change but they won't," Sam says firmly. "Those guys who already accept everyone will keep doing it. The others, well, me included, we don't even realize we're doing anything wrong."

"We *do* realize it!" Richard argues. "Else why would we say it's a bad habit like smoking? Those guys we see smoking, in the seventh grade? With all those signs around? They don't know it's bad to do it? Yeah, sure."

Julie peers at us over her glasses. "Here's what I think. If you knew how to act nicer you wouldn't need a rule. If you *need* a rule you won't stick with it."

Stephanie has been deciding whether to speak. Her arm has been darting up and down in tiny spurts. "I've got something to say, sort of about Amy's sister. Probably she didn't have this trouble in kindergarten, because some of the kids I played with then, in my other school, I probably wouldn't hang out with now. My mom says I've changed. Now I watch to see who the other kids accept. She doesn't like this."

"But wait!" Trish is on her feet. "Does this mean we were *kinder* in kindergarten? And now we're, like, the opposite of kindness? We didn't even think about all this stuff then and now we worry about it all the time. So is that the *opposite* of kindness because now it's so complicated and things worry you so much?"

Trish's voice trails off, but her idea is sharply defined. "The opposite of kindness?" I repeat. "Yes, that *is* what we've been talking about, isn't it? You're asking, were we kinder in kindergarten, when we didn't have to think much about it? We just naturally did it."

I push ahead. "What if we got in the habit of talking about this every day, the way we examine our sentences to see if the grammar is correct? Kindness and the opposite of kindness. Wouldn't we react more quickly when someone is being hurt? Wouldn't we become more sensitive to each other's feelings?"

"But how do you know we would?" Amy asks, more in curiosity than doubt.

"Why am I so sure? Because I've been watching young children most of my life and they are more often kind to each other than unkind. The early instinct to help someone is powerful. Think about it. How could this basic characteristic of ours disappear so quickly?"

The children wait for an answer. I take a deep breath and begin. "Let me tell you about a little boy named Teddy and some children in a London nursery school." I feel a surge of pleasure and optimism, knowing that my audience is about to hear a story that will remind them of who they were and can become again.

They will, of course, realize they have their own Teddy stories, those unheralded moments in time when we are witnesses to an act of kindness. The unkind voices that surround us are loud and shrill, demanding our thoughtful and truthful attention. All the more reason then to listen for the soft breath of friendship and carry our reassuring stories above the din. They are the beacons that help illuminate the moral universe. And we are required, even as is the great blue heron, to capture our prize and fly with it.